THE DASTARDLY BOOK FOR DOGS

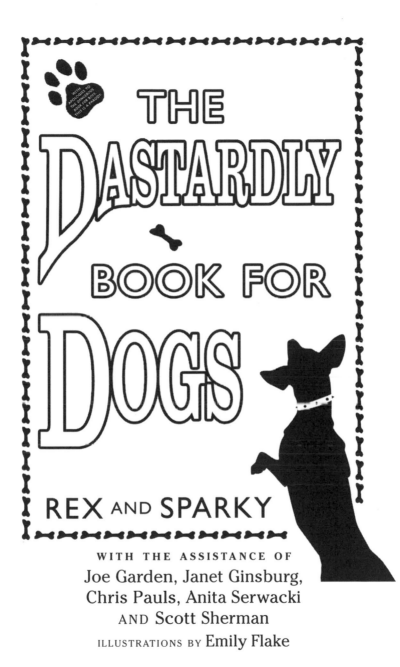

THE DASTARDLY BOOK FOR DOGS

WITH APOLOGIES TO THE DANGEROUS BOOK FOR BOYS. THIS IS A PARODY.

REX AND SPARKY

WITH THE ASSISTANCE OF
Joe Garden, Janet Ginsburg,
Chris Pauls, Anita Serwacki
AND Scott Sherman

ILLUSTRATIONS BY Emily Flake

HarperCollins*Publishers*

HarperCollins*Publishers*
77–85 Fulham Palace Road,
Hammersmith, London W6 8JB

The HarperCollins website address is: www.harpercollins.co.uk

First published in US by Villard Books,
an imprint of The Random House Publishing Group 2007
This edition published by HarperCollins*Publishers* 2007

1 3 5 7 9 10 8 6 4 2

Illustrations by Emily Flake

Design by *Semper Fido*

© Action 5, LLC 2007

A catalogue record of this book is
available from the British Library

ISBN-13 978-0-00-726730-9
ISBN-10 0-00-726730-4

Printed and bound in Italy by
L.E.G.O. SpA – Vicenza

Mixed Sources
Product group from well-managed
forests and other controlled sources
www.fsc.org Cert no. SW-COC-1806
© 1996 Forest Stewardship Council
FSC

For Marley

I Didn't Have This Book
When I Was a Puppy

There was a time not long ago when dogs were necessities, not accessories. We corralled wayward sheep in the heartland. We brought warming brandy to climbers in the hinterland. We were a valued asset to every fireman, a faithful sentinel for every rag-and-bone man and a slavishly loyal friend to everyman. We roamed freely because we had earned our keep, and our aggressions and wanderlust were celebrated, not curbed. It was a time when we ran on the ground instead of being toted about in frilly pink satchels, a time when we were simply hosed down in the garden instead of ferried to the groomer. It was a time B.D. – Before Domestication, when we could be what we are. Dogs.

In an age of pampering and pet steps, we seem to have lost touch with the greatest joys of canine existence – instinctive joys that the stoic Great Dane, the scampering Chihuahua and the barky old pound mutt alike could share: finding the nastiest odours to roll in, savoring the subtle earthy flavours of a Jimmy Choo slingback – and, of course, mounting bitches.

In these pages you will read great tales of canine bravery and bravado, such as the journey of the first dog to set foot on North America. You will know the glory achieved by courageous dogs of war. You will be awed by the landmark silver screen performances of Cujo, Old Yeller and the ferocious Beagle Pack in *Omen III: The Final Conflict.* You will know what it means to be a Dog.

What is the greatest scratching position in the world? How do you escape a humiliating attack of 'dressing up'? Can you ever catch your own tail? The answers are inside this book. We provide them not just as an instructional guide, but as a way to put you back in touch with your thrill-seeking, mischievous roots. Here we are reminded of the old canine proverb: '**Owwwwwwwwww, ow, ow, owwwwwww!**' – a sentiment as true today as it was in the day of our wild ancestors.

We wish we had a book like this when we were puppies. All too often we dogs are content to sleep seventeen hours a day, with a biscuit break here and there, unaware of all the wondrous fun we could be having treeing a squirrel, lapping up the wind from a car window or constructing a custom bed out of our owner's clean laundry.

When you reach a certain age, things become routine. The doorbell doesn't excite you as much as it once did, the bottoms at the park all smell the same, and your dreams of herding sheep on the open range have faded away.

But today's dog should never forget there's a whole wide world of adventure out there. We hope that this book doesn't merely remind you of your puppyhood, but truly rekindles it. **Owwwwwwwwww, ow, ow, owwwwwww**, indeed.

Contents

THE DASTARDLY BOOK FOR DOGS

Things You Can Chase

———————— ❖ ————————

Nothing breaks up the monotony of a boring day quite like a good chase. It's great exercise, excellent practice for eye-mouth coordination, and really, really fun. Chasing is also an ancient ritual of our species that directly led to many important cultural advancements, including fetch, bird-dogging and even doggy-paddling.

In practice, you can chase anything that moves: remote-control cars, toddlers, cats, imagined things – the list goes on and on. In order to keep the list manageable, we've only included the best inanimate chasing objects. We've left animals off this list to cover in greater detail later.

RULES

The golden rule of chasing is to never take your eye off of the chase thingy. Doing so will make you aware of all the other things around you that you could also be chasing, and you know what you end up catching when you try to chase two things at once? Nothing. And not catching something you are chasing is no fun, especially if what you're chasing is capable of laughing at you.

Frisbee

Of all the things you can chase, the Frisbee is the most entertaining. It seems to just hover in mid-air like a bird, but it's much easier to catch because it eventually comes down. You'll find that they're remarkably easy to sink your teeth into when you catch one. When your owner tries to reclaim it, don't let it go until the last possible moment. Caution:

A Frisbee's trajectory can waver, wobble and turn abruptly once air-borne depending on the wind and/or how much your owner throws like a girl. Never trust a Frisbee until it is firmly in your mouth, or else it is liable to quickly change course and smack you in the head.

Balls

The ball comes in two fun shapes: round and oval. Unlike a Frisbee, a ball tends to move erratically once it hits the ground, just like an animal. Great! Get a good sense of your terrain in order to anticipate the path a ball might take. For reasons dogs do not understand, balls seem to favour rolling down hills rather than rolling up them. The oval balls are hard to grab hold of unless they are made of soft foam, in which case you can really go to town and rip them to pieces. Round rubber or tennis balls bounce longer, and you can even catch them in mid-bounce!

Sticks

Sticks are just small pieces of tree, but they hold a very special place in dog–human history, as many believe they were the first objects thrown to canines by man. However, they aren't designed to travel very far. Mostly, they are good for playing fetch (see the chapter entitled 'The Formal Rules of Fetch'). Just be cautious. There are some stick-like objects that move and might even bite you. Remember this rule: If it tries to bite you, it is not a stick. It is a snake. Do not grab a snake.

Your tail

The great thing about your tail is that it is always there, ready for a good time. Even when you are in trouble for licking the steak and kidney pie and no one will play with you, your tail is up for being chased. It sits behind you, wagging, just asking you to go after it. If you are a breed that has a short tail, or no tail, or you had a tail and then lost it, this is obviously a challenge. In this case, you can substitute 'behind' for 'tail', even though it doesn't quite wag the same. The question then is whether you can catch it or not. The answer is that it doesn't matter. In this case the thrill is in the chase. And the chase is awesome.

Cars

PLEASE NOTE: This is for advanced chasers only. You cannot, nor should you, actually catch a car. They are terribly heavy, extremely uncooperative, and may actually cause you harm. That said, there's nothing more exciting than the feeling of running after a car. They are so fast and exciting! If one should actually stop and open the door for you, take stock of the situation. If you recognize the person as friendly, then by all means get in that car!

Treats

Obviously, if your owner throws one of these, don't bring it back to him. He'll think something's wrong with you.

A SPECIAL NOTE ON FAKE THROWS: Owners who fake-throw things for their own enjoyment are mean. If you are unfamiliar with the trick, here's how it works. Your owner will show you something extremely chasable, like a really nice ball. He will wave it in front of you until you are ready to rip it out of his hands, no matter what the consequences. Once he knows that he has your attention, he cocks his arm back as if he is going to throw it, except he doesn't actually let it go. This can lead to feelings of confusion and fear. You wonder: Where did the ball go? Is it chasing *you* now? Once you work out his trick, you should do all you can to condition him not to do it again by standing still and staring at him with your tongue hanging out. Eventually, he will feel bad and stop trying to fool you.

Begging:
A Primer

❖

'NO.' It's an ugly word, one we've all heard countless times before – whether we're jumping on a bed, tearing into a box of doughnuts or vigorously humping the leg of a visiting Chinese ambassador. But who among us wishes to heed it? And, quite simply – why should we?

Nowhere do we hear this word more often than at the dinner table. Begging ranks just below bowl feeding and above rubbish rummaging as a chief method of food procurement, but it requires a far more elaborate technique. If done correctly, it can yield a tasty morsel of man food. As such, it is broadly frowned upon by owners, who think of begging as a lowly and undignified way to comport yourself. Nothing could be further from the truth. If you are living in a home where begging is taboo, do not let that discourage you. Nothing short of banishment from the dining room should stop you, particularly if you are at a fancy party honouring the Chinese ambassador and there are cocktail sausages.

There are many styles, methods and schools of thought as to the most successful methods of begging. Dogs have debated this topic for ages, but, in the end, you must find the style that suits you best. Regardless of which style you choose, here are a few guidelines to follow.

CORRECT FORM

Posture

Is your head erect? Is your back straight? Are you seated comfortably enough to maintain this position throughout a five-course dinner?

Eyes

Many a meal is won or lost with a trick of the eyes. You may choose a docile, desperate or hopeful look, but whichever you choose, be sure to maintain eye contact with your owner. You are hypnotizing him. He must look directly into your eyes. He is under your control. He will give you the steak. He will . . . give . . . you . . . the steak. For best results, do not blink. Ever.

Ears

Your body doesn't stop at the top of your head, and neither should your technique. Always follow through with your ears. Floppy ears should extend out to the sides as much as possible. Pointed ears should remain high and sharp. Remember, good posture starts in the ears and ends in the toes. Use every inch in between to your advantage.

BE WATCHFUL

Eye contact is key, but do not be so focused on getting food directly from your owner that you

Be watchful at all times

miss an errant morsel that falls to the ground. While technically a table scrap, and not the direct result of begging, food falling in your line of sight is fair game. Move quickly before it gets tossed in the bin.

BE PATIENT, BE PERSISTENT

Begging often boils down to nothing more than a battle of wills, so you must persevere at all costs. Sometimes an unresponsive owner can be worn down with little more than a gentle nudge, a friendly pant or a soulful, uninterrupted stare.

Even the most experienced beggars among us have moments when we want to give up. It's at times like these that you need to ask yourself a question: Which is stronger? An owner's will? Or your desire for a succulent pork chop? Look deep into your stomach – you will find the answer.

STICK WITH PROVEN TECHNIQUE

Has it worked before? Then it WILL work again! If you have heard a 'no' but seen a 'yes', if you have been called a 'bad dog' but moments later had a piece of teriyaki chicken in your mouth – whatever you did was perfect, and will work again. And if it doesn't? . . .

TRY SOMETHING NEW

If you're not getting anywhere, and the dinner is disappearing quickly, try out a new technique. Put your paw on someone's lap, try your luck with the youngest person at the table, stand on your hind legs or cock your head that way you do. Whatever you choose, keep an open mind. You never know what's going to work until you try. Here are a few suggestions that have been proven to bring home the bacon:

Playing the dog's home puppy

We've all got a sad story to tell, if we only stop to think about it. A long-lost favourite chew toy. A night where you didn't get fed until 11 p.m. That time you got kicked out of bed. Whatever your sob story is, you can turn it into cold hard treats. Just be sure it's something your owner feels guilty about. Then chew on those heartstrings until things are in your favour.

Feigning injury

It's easy to goad your owner into handing over that Cumberland sausage. Mope around the house, add a slight limp to your gait and you'll be eating from the table in no time. Be careful not to overdo it. Anything too theatrical or hammy and they'll sense that you're faking it. You want to be convincing in a way that doesn't warrant too much concern, so don't fake anything too serious. The last thing you need is a surprise trip to the vet during the dinner hour. An injured paw is always plausible and usually easy to pull off.

Reverse psychology

This technique is brilliant and rewarding but difficult to employ. Say an entire roast turkey with dressing appears on the dinner table. You promptly trot out of the room, find a toy and pretend that you would rather be doing anything, anything at all, besides eating that delicious turkey that you don't even really care to taste. Act as if delicious golden-brown turkey bores you to tears, and that you cannot wait for your owners to be finished with their totally uninteresting tenderly roasted dinner with all the trimmings. Believe it or not, they will wonder where you are and why you aren't there begging at the table. Then they will come to find you and feed you. That's right – they will *bring the food to you*. Reverse psychology is a simple, effective tool that works wonders. Unfortunately many dogs find it physically impossible. It's worth a try, though. If you have the discipline, this one pays off handsomely.

While the time and energy invested in learning and executing begging techniques is high, the effort is low – and the pay-off rich and buttery. Remember: Stay strong, stay fast and stay put. Your owner loves you. Your owner is weak. Your owner will fold.

The Roots of Barks

Have you ever wondered how the barks we use every day came to be? Perhaps one day an ambitious pup will list the etymological roots of all the nearly 180,000 barks currently in use, but until that dictionary is written, here are the origins of some of our favourites.

Ruhruhruhruhruh. Meaning 'someone is at the door', this bark is derived from the ancient Indo-European barks 'rrrrrrr', meaning 'alert', and 'mmbuhmmbuh', meaning 'visitor'.

Ooowwww! Ooowww Asztalos, a Hungarian Kuvasz, is considered the first dog to identify the distance to the moon based on how long it took his howled name to bounce back to earth. After this landmark discovery, in 1379, Asztalos's first name became synonymous with moon-directed howls.

Grrrrr. The Grrrrrs were a pack of Pharaoh Hounds charged with sitting at the royal throne of Amenhotep IV (aka Akhenaten). Their job was to instil fear and humility in foreign envoys by emitting a low, threatening growl throughout the course of a visit with the pharaoh.

Woof. Though there is some debate about woof's etymological roots, it is generally accepted that the common greeting was first used in the early part of the fifth millennium when the Chinese refined animal-husbandry techniques. The Chinese would introduce themselves to their canine workers by saying, 'Wo-duh ming-d'zi …' ('My name is . . . '), and the dog would respond likewise, 'Wo-duh ming-d'zi . . . ' Over time, dogs learned to simplify their language for more efficient communication, and the greeting became shortened to 'wo-d'z', which in turn became 'woof'.

Arf. In Olde Bark, 'awrk' meant 'at the ready', which a dog would bark out at the beginning of a joust to signal the opposing riders to raise their lances. When the bark crossed the English Channel into France, 'awrk' became 'arf', and the meaning expanded. Today we use 'arf' to command an owner to lift a ball and prepare to throw it.

Ruff. Like many slang terms in our society, 'ruff' originated in the dog's home and was first popularized by inmates. Bad doggies in the Battersea Dogs' Home used the word around the keepers as part of a complex coded language. When a dog would plot an escape, he would mumble the word 'ruff' under his breath because it could be uttered with minimal jowl flapping (which keepers looked for as a sign of mischief afoot). The word is now used whenever a dog wants to skedaddle, even though an owner is content to stay in the house.

Yip! Yip! Yip! A relatively new bark, 'Yip! Yip! Yip!' derived from a Spanish bark that came into fashion quite circuitously. Queen Isabella II of Spain had an esteemed Ratonero Bodeguero Andaluz (translation: Andalusian Wine Cellars' Ratting Dog) named Rodrigo who suffered from a terrible stuttering problem. When the terrier would find a rat in the queen's wine cellar he would try to alert the cellar master in Spanish by saying, 'Aquí!' ('Here!'). Unfortunately all Rodrigo could muster was, 'Aq – aq – aq!' Rodrigo was embarrassed, but the queen loved her Ratonero Bodeguero Andaluz so much that she ordered all the dogs of Spain to bark with a stutter. Around the turn of the twentieth century, 'Aq – aq – aq' was crudely Anglicized into 'Yip! Yip! Yip!' but it remained the bark of choice for the dogs of heiresses and royalty alike.

Swimming

❖

Swimming is not a chore like bath time. Swimming is all about splashing around in cool water and enjoying the experience. Outdoor bodies of water might have some soapy suds like a bath, but there will be a lot more room to move about and have a good time, unlike when you're confined to a crummy tub.

Humans will swim on occasion because they need to. Maybe it's to get up to the bar for another drink, or because there's quite a bit of shiny money at the bottom of a fountain. Luckily we don't need to concern ourselves with understanding their rationale. All we care about is making sure that when they do go near water they let us get in and have a wild time.

Dogs should be careful not to enter the water immediately following a meal. Always wait a minimum of fifteen seconds after eating before swimming.

Entering the water can be accomplished in two ways: running or diving. Running into the water is fun but it isn't nearly as impressive as diving.

Diving involves jumping off solid ground, flying through the air and then landing in water. The best part is when you're in the air, so you should definitely take a quick look around.

A common launching-off point for a dive is called a dock, and usually you'll be entering a lake.

Swimming

In the event that you have the good fortune of swimming in a man-made pool, look for the diving board. Here you can bounce way up high and have ample hang time to execute a special dive.

We advise you to stick to diving in the traditional environments mentioned. It is not a good idea for dogs to dive off a cliff into the ocean, as some nutty humans do. Because we usually land on our bellies, a traditional dog dive from that high up will probably seriously injure or kill you. Only dogs with special training should ever attempt to enter the water from such a height. They employ an advanced technique taught by humans.

If you are in water where you can't touch the bottom, it's time to start swimming. If you do not begin swimming you will begin to sink, which is not good. No dog can breathe water. It's necessary to keep your head above it, and to accomplish this there is something called a 'stroke'.

The most common stroke was invented by dogs and is aptly named 'The Doggy Paddle'.

By employing a motion similar to running, you'll find that your nose will stay above water. A general rule is that the faster you move your legs the less you'll need to crane your neck to keep from going under. Just take care not to over-exert yourself and tire yourself out. Maintaining fluid leg motion will maximize your effort. It also gives the appearance that you have lots of swimming experience.

To go into reverse, employ 'The Backstroke', which is similar to 'The Doggy Paddle', but the other way.

Swimming

You might be wondering what you're supposed to be doing, or where to go when swimming. The answer is that you should go pretty well wherever your owner allows. It really isn't very different from on land. Swimming towards an object that will fit in your mouth is always good. Definitely stay away from personal watercraft that humans are riding or you might get run over by one. Often the drivers are waving to other people and may not see you. A lot of these people own convertibles on land and approach driving in water the same way.

After finishing your swim, get dried off. There's nothing more satisfying than shaking all that water from your coat.

If you're somewhere where the water smells funny and looks green, make sure to take a thorough stroll up and down the shore before it's time to go. There might be dead fish to roll in, and that's a great way to end your day.

Courageous Dogs in History – Part One

---❖---

We all have different ideas of what it means to be courageous. Some of us think that courage is physical, as when a fluffy Bichon Frisé stands up to a bossy Dobermann, or a Spaniel scares off an intruder. Some of us think it's mental, like when a defiant Sheepdog stretches out on the couch and flatly refuses to budge despite the pleas and threats of her owner. And some of us think it's a little bit of both, such as when you know you'll be punished for leaping over a lounge chair, stealing a plate of pork ribs and knocking Granny over in the process – but you do it anyway.

However you define courage, dogs have it by the bushel. Here are profiles of a few brave souls that make us proud to call ourselves canines.

TOGO AND BALTO: Sled Dog Heroes

In January 1925 the remote city of Nome, Alaska, was facing a deadly diphtheria epidemic. The people who lived there badly needed anti-toxin. Unfortunately, weather conditions were terrible. Temperatures had dropped to near fifty degrees below zero. That's cold enough to make you want to wear a hand-made dog sweater. In fact, it was so cold that the planes ferrying supplies to the isolated outpost couldn't make the trip (and the pilots were just too cold to get out of bed). Still, something had to be done. A great and wise decision was made by man that day – to enlist the services of his old friend, the dog. Togo and Balto were two of the dogs chosen to lead teams through the harsh terrain.

In what became known as the 'Great Race of Mercy', roughly 150 sled dogs carried the anti-toxin 674 miles in relays across the Alaskan

Togo   *Balto*

wilderness in sub-zero temperatures. They didn't wear booties. They
didn't stop for treats. They just ran. Fast.

Blizzard conditions meant that mushers sometimes could not see
their hands in front of them, or at least that's what they *said*. Mushers
are lazy. They say lots of things to get dogs to do more work. And what
good is a musher who can't even see where he's going? We bet Togo and
Balto both had half a mind to get up there in the sled and make the
mushers do the tough work for a change. Instead they just buckled
down and did what dogs do – the hard work. Fortunately for everyone,
the courageous canines were able to follow the trail's scent. They got
everyone back on track and conquered the dangerous terrain, complet-
ing the run in less than six days.

Balto, a Siberian Husky who was the lead sled dog on the final stretch
into Nome, became a canine celebrity. He went to all the red-
carpet events, and even got a statue in New York's Central Park. But many
feel that Togo, the lead Husky who ran the longest and arguably most difficult leg of the run, is the true hero of the event. There's no statue of
Togo, except in our hearts. We think that both of them are heroes.

PEG LEG PETEY, THE PIRATE DOG:
The Three-Legged Scourge of the High Seas;
The Most Terrible Terrier

NO MASTER FOR ME

A legendary pirate dog who would not hesitate to bite the scurvy Bulldogs of the Royal Navy, Petey was widely known as a goodly mutt – tolerant, high-spirited, brave and fearless despite his small size. It was a reputation he earned in one of the most famous adventure tales in all of dog lore.

Petey was only a wee stray when he was taken from the dead-end streets of London and shipped out to sea as a cabin pup, but he learned the laws of the deep blue quickly. Soon after leaving port, on a dark and stormy night, Petey's sloop was attacked by a great white whale. While others took shelter and the fierce storm waves tossed the captain overboard, little Petey stood his ground. He soon found himself engaged in a fierce and epic battle with the giant cetacean.

Even though he was a tiny dog, Petey had more courage, heart and cunning in his little body than most dogs and men twice his size. He jumped atop the great whale, sunk his teeth into its side and saved the sloop from certain destruction.

That night Petey lost his leg to the whale, but he gained something else – the respect of the ship's crew. Though he had little experience, he was voted captain and took to it like a natural. He was a magnanimous leader, commanding cats and dogs and men alike, and splitting his plunder of bones, treasure and treats fairly among all those in his crew.

Petey's life was not an easy one. There were no playful hikes in the canyons for him, and occasional walks on the plank were his only exercise. But his tales of high-seas daring and adventure inspire salty dogs and puppies alike to this day, and they will never be forgotten.

Courageous Dogs in History – Part One

A Connoisseur's Guide to Shoes

❖

Long ago, choosing a shoe was a simple affair. This is because there was originally only one kind of shoe. It was made of tar-coated leaves which were secured with knotted vines. This made for an adequate after-dinner *digestif,* but it was nothing to go on about. Eventually humans learned to cultivate shoes to have more palatable characteristics. For instance, the savoury clog was created by carefully combining the chewiness of a flip-flop with the hearty gusto of a work boot.

Today there are thousands of shoe varieties from a wide array of regions. Each has its own distinct aroma, texture and complexity of flavour.

With this broad palette to choose from, the connoisseur must determine which one is right to fit an occasion or one's prevalent mood.

Here are some favourites, covering many seasonal possibilities and owner budgets. We recommend all without reservation.

Jimmy Choo Crystal Accented Slingbacks: Delicate and with a pedigree, offers a gnawable two-inch heel, tender, earthy back strap and a band of Italian crystals on top which can be picked off and savoured individually. Be forewarned: Indulging in this shoe right before a wedding may come with repercussions.

Russell & Bromley Loafers: Enjoyment of this tasselled slip-on can be maximized by giving it a good soaking in the toilet for a time and then tucking it away in your shoe cellar to let it develop a musky richness. The true shoe-phile will enjoy deconstructing its complex leather weave.

Nine West Ballet Pump: With its simple, soft underside and light-bodied upper, this flat shoe's a perfect everyday choice. Its tidy front ribbon and springy elastic back add a surprise finish. Goes great with a dry biscuit.

Dolcis Wedge: The woven wedge heel has a light, breezy flavor, and its ankle wrap ribbon maximizes dragability. Winner of the 2007 Bournemouth Silver Chomp Award.

Animal Slippers: Synthetic materials are subtle at best but usually dull. Lack of flavour, however, is trumped here by the pure satisfaction of tearing one of these big, soft animal-shaped shoes apart. Their design and hearty texture provide a good dry run should you ever find yourself having to do battle with a real lion or monkey.

Bottega Veneta Fantasia Tropez Thongs: Perfect for an afternoon at your owner's friend's fancy holiday cottage. Its intricate metallic-front design has a rich bite and allows for good gripping. The decadent leather bottom gives this shoe a smooth, luscious balance.

Rugged Outdoor Sandals: This ambitious shoe features an intense trainer-like bottom and juicy sandal top. A flavour dynamo, with deep notes of Gold Bond. Appropriate for all occasions.

Off-brand Trainers: Opens with a heady bouquet of gym locker, revealing notes of Malaysian pleather. Relish its poor construction in late summer before school starts. Best savoured with an appreciative human child.

Ecco World Class Wing Tip GTX: Tear through its heady leather upper, but you'll be challenged by its waxed laces and reinforced interior. Cleats offer tyre-like chewing properties with lingering flavours of dirt.

SPECIAL NOTE TO CONNOISSEURS AND BEGINNERS ALIKE: There is one type of shoe you must leave untouched. This is the type with wheels coming out of the bottom. These shoes magically make your owner go much faster, turning a regular walk into a fantastic run!

Cats

Even if you have never seen a cat, you have heard the stories. They have nine lives. They crap in a box. They stare at you constantly. They fly when you aren't looking. They will turn you into a cat if they bite you during the full moon. Well, some of those are true, and others are less true. It is estimated by the Dog Estimation Bureau that some 35 per cent of all dogs have to share living quarters with a cat, despite the fact that they share few of the same values as dogs. Contrary to what some posit, cats are not our mortal enemies. On the whole they're just fussy and indifferent for reasons no one can understand. Cats are just a fact of life that we may as well get used to. To that end, here are some invaluable cat facts.

- First and most important, cats are weird.
- Cats startle pretty easily. These things startle a cat: barking, running, being licked, trying to play.
- Cats do not appreciate stinky things, so don't even try to share.

- Cats are constantly looking for things to scratch in order to keep their claws sharp so they can pop you one right on the nose.
- Cats can run very fast and crawl under places you cannot reach. Be careful not to hit your head trying to chase them.
- Cats do not like to be chased, even if they deserve it. They will often make this clear by popping you one right on the nose with their sharp claws if you try to chase them. Not fair!
- Cats do not honour territory. They will sleep in your favourite spot, even though cats are perfectly fine sleeping anywhere.
- Because cats are silent, they get away with things we would be punished for. For example, a cat can easily jump on the table and lick the sour cream off a potato until it hears your owner coming back. Then it scampers away, leaving you to take the blame for there being no sour cream on their potato. As if you'd ever eat delicious sour cream from a yummy potato!
- Cats take lots of naps. They do not like to be disturbed, and have been known to pop you one right on the nose with their sharp claws if you nudge them or bump them. Ouch!
- Cats spend a lot of time licking themselves, and not just their bottoms. All over.
- If you give a cat an earplug, it will bat it around for hours. If you give it a stick, it won't even get off the couch for it.
- Cats can sleep on their owner's beds whenever they want, even though they prefer to run around all night crashing into things.
- Cats refuse to do tricks, except for the aforementioned crapping in a box, which is pretty stupid, because then they do not have an excuse to go outside.
- Cats are very territorial about food. If you try to have a look at what they are eating, you may find yourself getting popped one right on the nose with their sharp claws, even if they are not interested in eating it. Hey!
- When a cat wants something, it will not bark. It will make another noise.

If your owner inexplicably brings one of these animals home, don't even ask why. They don't seem to be much good for anything, and thinking about it can drive you crazy. Instead of trying to work out why you now have to share a water dish with some sulky disobedient animal, you should spend that time brushing up on them. The best policy for those who have to live with cats is to avoid them altogether. Unfortunately, this is not always possible. Your food bowl will probably be close to the food bowl of the cat, and, let's face it, it's hard to avoid an animal that is competing for affection and occupying the same indoor space as you. The following pointers are a good introduction to peacefully coexisting with a cat.

- Don't bark your displeasure. Barking will only annoy your owners, and you will be scolded. Don't make cats look good by comparison.
- Your owner will always take the side of the cat. Wait until he is gone to give a cat the business, then pick it up in your jaws. Don't clamp down. This will remind It who the boss is.
- If you come across a cat who looks as though it stuck its paw in a light socket and sounds like a balloon leaking, back away slowly or you could end up getting popped right on the nose with its sharp claws!

- There are times, and they are rare, when you will be lying on your side and a cat will walk right up and lie down next to you, nuzzle up and go to sleep. You should enjoy this peaceful moment, because a few awkward minutes with a cat can get you months of lighter punishment if this cute little scene is witnessed by your owner. This is worth double if he takes a picture.

If you are still having a hard time with all this, just remember that as much as you like to sleep, cats like to sleep even more, giving you some well-deserved time to romp freely. Romp as much as you want.

Building a Kennel

❖

Inside has its upside. It's usually an agreeable temperature, features many comfortable places to nap, and is, of course, the location of your food bowl. The downside is, when you're indoors, there's no way to really know what's happening outdoors. Think about it. This very second, sticky new pine cones could be falling from the sky or a squawky jackdaw might be making a racket with impunity. How would you know? You wouldn't! Not when you're inside, anyway.

Is there some way to bring the benefits of indoor living outside so you can keep an eye on things in comfort? Absolutely! It's called a kennel and building one of your own is easy.

These steps will lead you on the path to dog home ownership and peace of mind.

Step 1. Pick the spot where you want your kennel. It should be prime territory with clear views of garden entry points such as the gate, large trees, and the dark space under the veranda. It must be prominent enough to show potential intruders that you own the place, but just secluded enough to allow for an element of surprise when confronting a trespassing squirrel or errant party balloon. Once you've chosen your site, take care not to do your business in that general area. Then begin the process of turning that patch of lawn into dust by digging, running in circles and lying there all afternoon. This is your foundation, so invest some time and don't cut corners.

Building a Kennel

Step 2. Once you conceive a design and begin assembling materials, you will quickly realize that you possess neither carpentry skills nor an opposable thumb to operate the required tools. These things make kennel construction possible. You must now secure the assistance of your owner.

Step 3. Next time you are brought back inside, have a snack, then immediately begin barking to be let outside again. Your owner will ignore you at first, but persistence will reap benefits.

Step. 4. You should now find your outdoor time readily increasing. When this occurs, park yourself on your foundation while looking mournfully at your owner's home. If it's raining or really hot when you're let out to do your business, don't be eager to scratch on the door for re-entry. Just sprawl out on your foundation and look really pathetic. Put on the saddest eyes you've got. Make it clear that you really, really like that spot and you wouldn't be so miserable if there was some sort of shelter available there. Repeat until your owner heads to the DIY superstore.

Step 5. Congratulations! You have a beautiful new kennel!

How to Escape
Humiliating Costumes

❖

However much you wish to please your owner, you must put your paw down when it comes to costumes. Being dressed in a studded biker helmet and a pair of vinyl chaps demeans you both. If your owner insists on putting you in one of these costumes, bark twice, aggressively, to voice your displeasure. If he is unable or unwilling to listen, you must do everything within your power to escape from the outfit at once.

Remember, it is not disrespectful or disloyal to escape from a ridiculous outfit. In fact, it is imperative you do so immediately. Otherwise you will most assuredly be photographed, the photographs will surface on the Internet, and you will have little chance of ever recovering your dignity.

It is of the utmost import that you destroy the outfit post-escape. This cannot be stressed enough. You need to send a bold message to your owner, which is that you prefer the noble, comfortable costume you were born with to that of a mermaid, policeman, or lobster.

Techniques for escaping several 'popular' costumes follow.

REINDEER

This common seasonal humiliation is fairly simple to escape; all you have to do is work free of the awkward antler headdress. To do this:

1. Bow your head until the antler tips are touching the floor.
2. Work the antlers into the ground. (See fig. A.)

Fig. A

3. The antlers should fall from your head. Pick them up, take them outside, and quickly bury them in a neighbouring garden. (See fig. B.)

Fig. B

Alternative technique: Run full speed throughout the house. Steer the antlers into valuable dishware and through tall stacks of important papers. Do not stop until after you have heard your owner screaming. He should remove them quickly.

ELF

The holidays are rife with costuming dangers. Those fortunate enough to escape the loathsome reindeer outfit should not gloat too quickly, lest they find themselves outfitted in the dignity-robbing elf costume. The elf is a mess of green felt and buttons. Depending on the complexity of the costume, you may suffer the additional embarrassments of a 'jolly' red cap, bells that 'jingle-jangle' or a shiny black belt which holds up purely imaginary trousers. Either way, you will look like a Year Two art project unless you make short work of this costume. Thankfully, if you have ever employed a vertical surface to scratch an itch, you can escape this costume with little difficulty. We suggest the following techniques:

1. Find a solid, free-standing object or a sturdy wall where you can work unobserved by your costumer.
2. Begin rubbing the costume against the wall, slowly at first, and then more forcefully. At the same time, use your paw to tug the bottom of the costume towards the floor.

3. The snaps holding the felt costume around your shoulders should give, freeing you.
4. If you are wearing a cap, you may use the removal techniques listed above (for antlers) or below (for hats). (See fig C.)

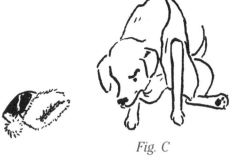

Fig. C

Important Note on Accoutrements

If you are wearing bells, you MUST slip out of these PRIOR to your escape attempt! Bells telegraph your every move, and if you are to succeed in your escape you need to perform these manoeuvres in secrecy. Slip them off your paws as quickly and quietly as possible before proceeding.

When you have removed both parts of the costume, resume with the final step:

5. Shred the costume thoroughly. We suggest ripping each item into at least thirty-two smaller pieces. (See fig. D.) Chew on it, drool on it, but whatever you do, be thorough. You want to ensure that felt never touches your fur again.

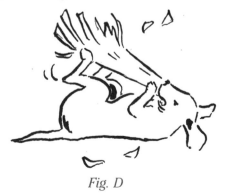

Fig. D

ZORRO

This humiliating outfit presents the twin challenges of hat and cape. Mastering the cape escape is a difficult task, but one well worth knowing. You can expect to encounter the cape again in Superman, Pimp Dog and most Elvis costumes.

Fig. E

1. Locate the draw strings, generally found under the muzzle, which allow your owner to tighten or loosen the cape. (See fig. E.)
2. With your paw, bat the string into your mouth. This will take some effort.
3. Pull on string. The cape will fall to the floor.
4. To remove the hat, rub your head furiously against a piece of furniture until the hat is knocked entirely askew. Continue, working the hat free from your head, until it is on the floor.
5. Urinate on hat. Urinate on cape. (See fig. F.)

Fig. F

HIPPIE

This costume is essentially nothing more than a brightly coloured, modified elf costume, but it's far more degrading. You'll want to remove the hat and wig first. Unless you have previous experience with Velcro, the rest of the outfit will take more time.

1. Lie on your back.
2. Wriggle and nip at the outfit. Remember to use your teeth – they're your best resource. If you hear what sounds vaguely like a bag of treats opening as the outfit loosens, you're doing well. (See fig. G.)
3. With your dominant paw, bat at the hat/wig until it goes over your ears and off your head.
4. Defecate on wig. (See fig. H.)

Fig. G

Fig. H

Epic Walks – Part One
The Land Bridge

❖

Thousands and thousands of years ago a land bridge spanning what is today the Bering Strait brought an unprecedented migration of animals and humans from Asia to North America. Of the many treacherous treks, perhaps none were as epic and important as the one made by Mikmik, the first dog ever to set foot on the North American continent.

Mikmik resembled a modern-day Malamute, but like many of our primitive ancestors he had several physical characteristics no longer seen in the breed. For example, Mikmik had blue (not brown) eyes, was twelve feet tall, and had three-foot tusks. Mikmik lived a peaceful life in eastern Siberia with his Mahlemut Inuit family. He hunted arctic lions and sea monsters with the men, rolled in the snow with the kids, and even aided the women in stitching together fine sealskin parkas. This was Mikmik's life: simple, serene, and pretty cold, since he was in Siberia during the Ice Age.

The morning of the landmark walk began quite unassumingly. Mikmik's owner clapped a few times and enthusiastically asked, 'Want to go out, boy? Do you? Want to go out?'

Mikmik darted for the door of the igloo to indicate that, yes, he did in fact want to go out. His owner grabbed the polar-bear-sinew lead, and off they went. Normally Mikmik and his owner had a standard route they stuck to: head up to the big glacier, toss the narwhal tusk around for a little bit, and then back home. That morning, however, Mikmik's owner had an argument with the wife about spending too much time clubbing seals and not enough time with the kids, and because of the row Mikmik's owner really needed to let off some steam.

'I'll tell you what, boy,' said Mikmik's owner. 'Why don't we head east today – try something new?'

Mikmik was all for it. Recently Mikmik had noticed that a bunch of the wolverines, sabre-toothed lynx, wooly mammoths and giant short-faced bears he usually chased on walks weren't around any more.

As they strolled along, Mikmik's owner began airing his marital woes. 'She just – oh, she doesn't understand me sometimes, you know? It used to be just us – just me and her, and that was great. But now with the kids and the food scarcity – there's a ton of pressure on me that I'm not sure I can deal with. Oh, did I tell you she wants to move? She says we need more space, as if I can afford a bigger place with the amount of walruses I'm bringing in.'

Mikmik loved his owner, but the endless rambling stream of complaints about domestic life was becoming annoying. Still, they had now been walking for a solid two hours and Mikmik didn't want to wreck this great walk, which is exactly what would happen if he told his owner that it was time to face facts, recognize he's not a sixteen-year-old any more, and accept his new identity as a family man with obligations.

After another hour of griping and moaning, Mikmik's owner sighed, looked up at the sun to check the time, and said, 'OK, boy, we'd better head back. I don't want to get shouted at again for not shaving down the ice in the front garden. Do your business, Mikmik. Come on, boy. Pee-pee time.'

It took a while for Mikmik to find a good spot. He had never been out this far east, and picking a single spot to mark among all this new territory was an overwhelming decision. Finally, Mikmik found a good area right in the middle of what he assumed was a solid piece of snow-covered land. He lifted his leg and let loose a hearty flood of urine. As the hot torrent splashed against the ground, one thing suddenly became abundantly clear: Mikmik and his owner were standing on ice.

A vast crack spread instantly across the land bridge and Mikmik and his owner found themselves on the eastern side of a crevasse. The twelve-foot-tall canine's fluids had caused an enormous rift in the ice sheet, and the distance was too great for Mikmik or his owner to jump over. Mikmik had never felt so ashamed in his life. He tucked his tail between his legs and lowered his head before his owner, which didn't really work because his head was still a good six and a half feet above his owner.

Epic Walks – Part One: The Land Bridge

Mikmik's owner shrugged, knowing his friend didn't cut the two of them off from the other side of the world on purpose. 'It's OK, boy. Let's go and find out what else is on this side of the planet, and we'll go back home once this spot freezes over. I could use the holiday anyway. Would you like that, Mikmik? Eh? Would you?'

Mikmik panted with delight and the two continued on their walk. About two days later the pair stumbled upon one of the most magnificent sights ever seen by man or dog. The glacial trail they had been walking on suddenly gave way to rolling steppes teeming with all the wildlife that used to inhabit Siberia, plus all sorts of new animals that looked as though they might be really tasty. It was Alaska, and it held a bounty unlike anything Mikmik could have imagined. Also, land prices were super low since there were no other humans around.

Mikmik and his owner knew they had found a new home for their Mahlemut family, and they hurried home to round up the wife and kids. Three weeks later they returned to Alaska and became the first home-owners in the New World.

Interpreting Commands

———✧———

All humans talk to a dog at some point in their lives.

Those who live alone tend to confer with us because they have no one else. Others have lots of people around but are chatty and like to be talking constantly, even if no one is paying attention. A few actually expect us to participate in the conversation. We recommend steering clear of these people.

No matter what the situation, you should always listen when your owner talks to you. He's trying to say something.

However, there is a difference between talking that is conversational and that which is meant to be authoritative. It's usually pretty easy to distinguish between the two. Obviously if you're on the table eating the flowers, it's a good guess that you're in big trouble, because you're on the table eating the flowers.

Things become more complicated when humans, specifically owners, don't always mean exactly what they say. An order you interpret as being angry or negative may not be so at all, and may just be their awkward way of reacting to something else.

So how can you tell what's really going on? What should you do? See opposite for a list of situational commands and recommended responses.

YOU	OWNER	THEY SAY	YOU SHOULD
Wrapped affectionately around owner's leg	Just out of shower, dripping wet	'Stop it.'	Stop. Wait until he puts on pyjamas or gets dressed for work.
It is Sunday, 8:59 p.m., GMT, and you would like to play	Sitting in easy chair with big glass of lemonade	'Where's your ball? Go and find your ball.'	Locate your ball, but don't bring it back until 10:01 p.m., when *Battlestar Galactica* is over.
Romping in operating room	About to perform initial incision for open-heart surgery	'Go on, out.'	Take a walk down to the cafeteria.
Jumping up and licking faces of uniformed children	Listening to Boy Scout Troop Leader explain how much money they need to raise for jamboree	'Down.'	Continue playing until owner makes quick donation, pulls you inside, and shuts door.
Pulling on lead	Pulling in opposite direction	'Hold on.'	Evaluate whether whatever you want to get is worth not being able to breathe.
Trying to go outside with owner despite how he smells	Leaving house after dousing himself with stuff that makes him smell funny	'No.'	While he's gone, find whatever made him smell so foolish and destroy it completely.
Were just about to bolt after something in the bushes	Staring at you	'[Your Name].'	See if he says it again, otherwise take off.
Would very much like to know what's behind all that cardboard on the windows	Trying to enter adult video/gift shop and surprised to find you there	'Go home.'	Pretend you're heading home, then slip inside when the man sitting in his car goes in.

Poo: An Indelicate Discussion

❖

We all get a little confused about our bodies from time to time. We love to eat food, but some four to eighteen hours later we begin to undergo a change. We start to feel urges we didn't have before, urges to go outside and squat down to expel something from our behinds. That something is poo, and it is totally natural.

Some dogs are embarrassed by the fact that they have to poo, and even conflicted by their feelings about poo. Let's make one thing clear right off the bat: Every dog poos. It's not weird or embarrassing. It's natural. Pooing is just a fact of life. The thing you have to remember is that it is more than a reason to clean your arse. Here are some of the most common questions about poo.

WHAT IS IT?

As indicated before, poo is what's left when your body re-moves certain materials from food. Once gone, the remaining matter acquires a much more pungent and interesting odour.

WHY DO WE HAVE TO GO OUTSIDE TO DO IT? WHAT IF I CAN'T WAIT?

You don't *really* have to. It's not as if it's impossible to poo in-doors. It's just frowned upon by owners. Remember this: It's not your fault. It's your owner's, and if you poo on a carpet, the odds are good that your owner will not come home late again.

As for *why* we have to go out-side, as hard as it is to believe, people do not like poo. They find its odours and textures to be unpleasant. Perhaps if they took the time to actually touch it, re-ally smell it, they would appreci-ate it the way dogs do. But no, they always use plastic bags or huge metal tongs to pick it up as soon as it comes out of us.

WHY DO HUMANS PICK UP OUR POO IF THEY DISLIKE IT SO MUCH?

No one can really tell. They don't like to talk about it. All we know for sure is that they wrinkle their noses and turn their heads when they stoop down to take it away. One theory is that there is some kind of social pressure to pick it up so they can compare with other owners and brag about how great their dog is. Another theory is that they are sending it to France, where they scatter it all over the streets and pavements.

WHERE SHOULD WE POO?

You should poo wherever you like. Some people try to get you to walk off the pavement and into the oily, grimy, hot gutter. That's nasty. Instead of letting them dictate your duty, try pooing on tree roots, on the pavement, or in a tall patch of weeds. Just poo where your mood moves you. What does it really matter, anyway? Your owner will clean it up.

CAN WE EAT ANOTHER DOG'S POO?

Absolutely! It's a great way to find out what dogs have been hanging around, and what they have been eating, and it is all part of being a well-adjusted, sociable dog. Just remember that your owner will likely try to prevent you from doing so at all costs. If he sees you eating poo, it will be a long time before he lets you lick his face. Do not let this stop you. Just wait until his back is turned and gobble that poo up. Sneakily-eaten poo tastes all the sweeter.

Humans have an expression: 'Poo happens.' As silly as it sounds, it is absolutely true. Don't try to stop it, or hide it. Go out and let it fly. It's all a part of how we're made. 'Poo happens.' Let it happen to you.

Escaping Fenced-in Areas

———❖———

Every dog wonders why humans put fences around their gardens. The rationale given by owners varies:

'It's so you don't run off and get hit by a car.'
'We like to know exactly where you are.'
'Because we want to.'

They may not state it the same way, but they are all essentially saying the same thing: 'We're in control here.'

Using some tried-and-true techniques, a dog can defy its owner and taste sweet freedom. However, all dogs must ask themselves if escaping is actually necessary, or even wise. Remember, if you escape there will probably be consequences. If your garden is adequately sized, you may opt to just hang out and work the lawn down to bare earth.

A successful escape can result in a search party, made up of your owner and some local kids who will probably find you in a short period of time, especially if you like the neighbour's garden. Your owner will be very unhappy, and punishments for escaping are typically severe. Life will get harder on the inside. If you value garden time, stay put.

But if the fence is just too much to look at any longer, or if you see escape as the only thing between you and as much fun as you can have in twelve to sixty minutes, then there are two basic ways to defeat a garden fence – going over or going under it.

GOING OVER

A garden fence can be made out of metal or wood, but both varieties are usually standard at neck-high on an owner. This is too tall for any dog to clear under his own power. Instead, look for stuff near the fence. If either of these items is nearby you might be in business:

You should be able to get over easily enough using these objects as launching points if they are within two or three feet of the fence. If both are available, consider employing them in sequence.

Another method of going over requires an accomplice and is not possible if you are the only dog in the garden. The accomplice boosts you up on top of the fence, where you can jump to the other side. This can be done a couple of different ways.

One last thing to remember is that if you're going over, take care to have an idea what's on the other side of the fence. Do as much advanced reconnaissance as possible before executing the escape. The last thing you need is to land on top of a greasy sunbather or a larger dog.

GOING UNDER

If going over is not practical or doable, investigate the possibilities of going under. This method of escape plays to your natural instinct to dig, only instead of a straight-down hole you will be working on creating a trench beneath the bottom of the fence.

Once completed, simply enter the trench and crawl under the fence. If you find it is not large enough, stop immediately and resume digging. *Do not* try to force yourself through a space that is undersized. You can become stuck.

Recently dogs have encountered a type of fence that doesn't make much sense. Even with no visible physical barrier in front of them, many dogs have reported instant, terrible pain when attempting to leave the garden that only stops upon backing up. It is not completely understood how this new type of fence works, but the consensus among most dogs is that it must have something to do with the collar, since that's where the pain originates from.

There may be only one way to defeat this fence, and it will not be easy. If you have a kennel, begin your tunnel there and place a blanket over the hole so it is not discovered. We advise working exclusively at night and confiding in no one.

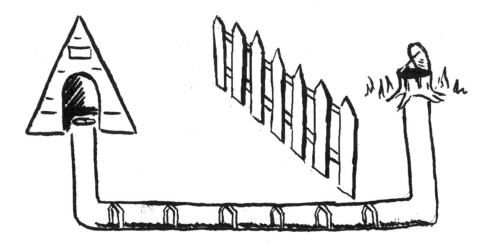

Should you escape successfully, time will tell if life on the outside is right for you. Four hours is usually enough. If you miss your creature comforts, then make your way home.

It's hard to walk back through the front door, but your owner will be happy to see you and probably dismiss all charges.

Great Dog Battles –
Part One

That dogs like to play is a given. However, in these times of endless doggy leisure, it is easy to forget that dogs can also be fierce warriors. Here we celebrate the stories of dogs who engaged in battles, not for glory or the mere act of fighting, but for the betterment of dogkind. While no dog enters a battle lightly, these stories are a good reminder that a dog – any dog – can rise to the occasion with acts of bravery and heroism.

BUSTER SANDERSON V. THE POSTMAN

A.D. **1993.** The rivalry between dogs and postmen is as old as dog history itself. From the menu distributors of the Phoenician empire to the parcel delivery service representatives of today, dogs have long fought to protect their owners from these sinister bearers of envelopes and packages.

In the Midlands town of Willenhall, relations between dogs and postal workers were tense, with dogs being tethered or shut inside, and postmen and women flaunting their satchels without a care. This one-sided peace did not sit well with Buster, the Sanderson family's four-year-old terrier. For

Buster Sanderson, Hero Dog

years, the postman would casually come up the garden path and slide the post into a slot in the door. Buster was powerless to do anything but watch the post fall to the floor and bark at his unseen enemy, day after day.

All this changed when the Sandersons installed a doggie door, giving Buster the new tactical advantage of unfettered access to both the front and back gardens. Rather than rush out unprepared, he used the time to draw up a comprehensive battle plan. For the next two weeks, he took every opportunity to study the terrain of the front garden, analyse the fence and gate, and see where he could gain the most strategic advantage. He also listened for the clicking sounds of the postman unlatching the gate and coming up the path, looking for any sign of weakness. He realized that the postman usually came at the same time, around 11:00 a.m., and that he latched the gate after him. A tragic error. Now all Buster had to do was to set the trap.

On a crisp autumn day in October, Buster nudged the dog door open at 10:50. He trotted around the perimeter to clear the area of squirrels and blackbirds that might distract him from his mission. There would only be one chance to strike, and with no reinforcements to back him up, the success of this operation fell solely on his shoulders. Having satisfied himself that nothing had changed since 8:58 a.m., Buster took his position in the natural camouflage of the bushes by the front door and waited. When the postman had not shown up by 11:02, Buster became nervous. 'Did someone tip the postman off?' he worried. 'What if he brings a whole army of postmen?' Buster almost backed out before realizing that this was just one of the postman's crafty psychological-warfare tactics designed to weaken his resolve.

At 11:07, Buster heard the infernal whistling of the postman approaching. He knew the battle was upon him.

When the postman opened the gate and walked up to the door, Buster screwed up his courage and made his move. With a mighty yip, Buster lunged at the postman, causing him to fall backwards and drop

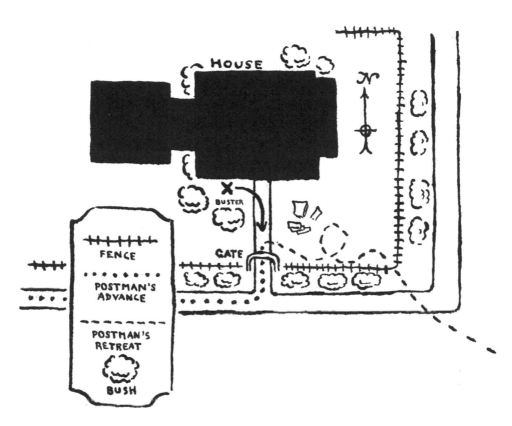

Buster's Battle Plan

the post he was about to deliver. He was quick to recover, however, and reached into his pocket for a treat, which he threw on the ground at Buster's feet. Buster could not be bought off his mission so easily. He let the postman know this fact by uttering a series of yelps that would have struck terror in a normal man. This, though, was a postman, and not normal in the slightest.

The postman gathered his envelopes, stood up, and continued walking towards the door.

Buster was dumbfounded. How could a person be so brazen? It was time for him to unleash the mother of all battle tactics. When the postman's back was turned, Buster sprang up and launched himself into the air, aiming right for the postman's meaty behind. The postman yelled and shouted, but Buster retained a firm grip on his trousers. Realizing his defeat, the postman dropped the envelopes and scrambled out of Buster's garden.

It was time to bask in the glory of victory. The postman had been routed, and Buster had trophies from his battle: a 2" x 2" piece of cloth from the seat of the postman's trousers, and an Argos catalogue to chew on.

While the postman was obliged by law to return to the house, he did so only after a post-war accord mandating that the Sandersons place a postbox at the end of the garden path, thereby ensuring that the postman would never set foot on Sanderson property again.

From that day forward, it was obvious to one and all that the garden belonged to Buster.

Questions about the World

Q: Why is there only one dinnertime a day?

A: Wise dogs have pondered this throughout the ages, yet we remain baffled. Recorded history shows us that, in fact, the number of times people eat during the day has varied widely in different cultures and eras. Some eras have seen people eating a 'midday meal', a 'luncheon', and both a 'dinner' and a 'supper' all in the same day, while others have barely eaten an evening meal at all!

Sadly, while dogs have tirelessly and peacefully lobbied for additional meals also called 'dinner', their efforts have failed repeatedly. This is why most modern canines have shifted our focus to how *much* we can consume at dinner and what it is we're eating. Dogs who are able to quickly consume their entire meal and still surreptitiously beg significant table scraps or treats may be considered to get two dinner meals a day, but this situation is rare and is the exception rather than the rule.

Q: Why do people
   wear clothes?

A: Take a good, long look at your
   favourite human. You'll notice
   lots of things about his appearance that are dissimilar to
   yours. His ears are ugly. His
   snout is small, dry and practically useless; his hands,
   spindly and awkward for digging. You'll also notice one
   overwhelming difference: his
   total lack of fur. Sure, he's got
   body hair, and maybe even a
   little on the face, but it's
   hardly enough to do him any
   good, and even then he's constantly removing it. As far as
   we can tell, men and women
   clothe themselves for protection against the elements,
   which they need, due to their
   aforementioned lack of real
   fur. But they also do it for the
   same reason they're afraid to
   do a poo out in the open:
   They're easily embarrassed.
   People will often turn bright
   red when they discover their
   teats are visible, and they are
   definitely not comfortable ex-
   posing their genitals.

Q: If a northbound train travel-
   ling 300 miles at a speed of
   120 m.p.h. leaves the station
   at 3 p.m., and another head-
   ing south 100 miles to Leeds
   at approximately 70 m.p.h.
   passes that station at
   2 p.m.,which train will
   arrive first?

A: Trains certainly are fun to
   bark at.

Q: Which train is serving
   steak and kidney pie?

A: The westbound train is
   serving a delightful steak and
   kidney pie accompanied by
   creamy mashed potatoes,
   julienned vegetables and a
   serviceable cabernet.
   Assuming a six-ounce serving
   of steak and kidney pie and
   approximately 400 passengers, if the train continues at
   its current speed you should
   be able to smell it for exactly
   24 minutes – before, during,
   and after it passes through
   your town.

Q: Why can't I drink from the water bowl in the toilet?

A: Have you wondered why someone would sit on their water bowl? People do it all the time. We can only guess that people are naturally very territorial about their wonderful porcelain bowls – which are miraculously filled with fresh cool water – as any one of us would be. This habit would also explain why they become so angry when we enjoy a drink from it ourselves, because although people have been observed sitting on it, reading on it, cleaning it and occasionally hugging it, no person has ever been observed drinking from it. That said, you can do whatever you like as long as nobody sees you do it.

Q: Where do humans go all day?

A: None of us likes to be left alone. The mind begins to wander: *Where is my owner? This is just like him. He does this every Monday to Friday. Is he in the park? Is he with another dog? Did he go for a walk? I'll bet he did. When will he be home? Is he having fun without me?*

You'll be relieved to hear that the answer to that last question is a resounding 'no'. Your owner is at work, which is like a boarding kennel for humans. More than likely, he is sitting in a small cube-shaped space for approximately eight hours, taking orders from his 'boss', or Alpha, being generally submissive and thinking about how badly he wants to go home. He is not particularly happy about it, but he does enjoy socializing with fellow workers, sneaking a nap when his boss is not in, and taking advantage of unlimited coffee refills. His reward for going is a little bit of money to spend on you, his one and only, whom he is always happy to come home to. Greet him warmly.

Q: **Who's a good boy?**
Who's a good boy?

A: It is a question as old as the mountains and the trees. *Who is a good boy?*

When you stop to think about it, what do the words *'good',* or *'boy',* or *'who is a'* really even mean? Indeed, the world is rarely as simple as 'good' or 'bad', both being unreal absolute concepts that only have meaning in relation to one another. Most of us demonstrate complex moral behaviours that could hardly be labelled consistently 'good' or 'bad': we exhibit heroism one moment and cowardice the next; alter-

nately biting and licking the very hands that feed us. And none of us would be so foolhardy as to argue for a moment that we are 'boys' – that term clearly refers exclusively to the immature male offspring of *Homo sapiens,* and does not accurately describe any member of the canine community.

Perhaps the only real answer is 'none of us'. None of us is unequivocally 'good', none of us is a 'boy', and none of us can truthfully claim to be a 'good boy'.

Or, the answer is you. Yes it is! It's YOU! You are a good boy! You are a very good boy!

How to Pick a Pill out of Peanut Butter

———❖———

One of the most wonderful sounds in the world is that of a peanut butter jar being unscrewed. With a splendid mixture of stickiness, nutty flavour and an aroma that lingers on your tongue for days, peanut butter might be the perfect food. But its deliciousness can be easily abused. Due to its unique viscosity, many owners will hide revolting medicine deep in the core of a peanut butter ball. How do you know if your peanut butter has a pill inside it? Take this simple test. Is your owner giving you peanut butter? If the answer is yes, then the chances are good that there is a pill in it.

Pills come in a variety of flavours, including horrible, terrible, awful and repulsive. Accidentally biting a pill hidden in peanut butter will utterly ruin what should be one of the greatest gastronomic experiences you will ever have. Plucking out a pill is a delicate art that requires patience and great dexterity, but the effort is worth it.

Since the process of pill extraction is somewhat time consuming, do a quick sight test to see if your owner might simply be having a moment of weakness and is giving you 'people food' for non-nefarious reasons. If it's around 2 a.m., your owner is wearing nothing but his underwear and is staring vacantly into the refrigerator, you might be getting some pill-free peanut butter.

How to Pick a Pill out of Peanut Butter

The moment peanut butter is presented to you in a moulded ball form, be careful. Research indicates an over 99.99 per cent likelihood that spherically delivered peanut butter holds a nasty surprise.

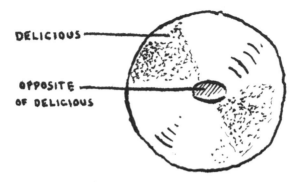

Inner layers of a peanut butter ball

To remove a pill from peanut butter you will need:
- a hard, clean surface
- an accessible potted plant
- water, preferably warm, *definitely* not from your water bowl.

METHOD

1. When the ball of peanut butter is presented, grip it with your teeth. DO NOT let the ball touch your tongue! Even the lightest smack of peanut butter will send you into an uncontrollable licking fit that will inevitably end in a taste disaster. Control is key.

2. With the ball firmly gripped, tip over the potted plant. Put lots of force into it so that the spread of soil is as wide and long as possible. For pill extraction to be successful, it must take your owner at least six minutes to clean up the mess.

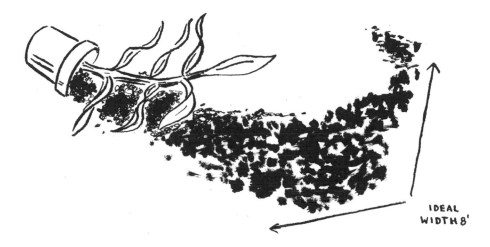

IDEAL
WIDTH 8'

3. While your owner is distracted with the plant, drop the ball on a clean surface. Kitchen or bathroom tiles work best. Spread the peanut butter in a straight line with your paw until the pill is revealed. Don't worry about peanut butter getting stuck in your paw. It makes for an excellent licking experience later.

How to Pick a Pill out of Peanut Butter

4. Again, using only your teeth, carefully pick up the pill. Drop the pill into warm water and vigorously splash the water until it is completely dissolved. Do not dissolve a pill in your water bowl as the taste may embed itself on the lining and permanently ruin future drinks for you. Toilets are ideal for dissolving pills since the water supply is regularly flushed, but pools and hot baths work as well.

Dissolving the pill is essential to the process, as it is the only way to ensure your owner won't try to give it to you again. Simply hiding the pill allows for the possibility of your owner finding it and making you ingest it without the aid of peanut butter. The pill must be destroyed. After you've accomplished this final step, return to your peanut butter spread and enjoy.

Foul Smells Every Dog
Should Roll in

Ever seen a fly-swarmed pile of rubbish in the park and had the urge to dive right in? Of course you have. The temptation of week-old mustard is just too powerful to resist. What you probably don't know is that your genetic programming compels you to smell bad. Today, spinning around in a mound of refuse will probably get you banished to the garden, but historically, reeking – and reeking on purpose – was very practical and important.

Our lupine forebears had both survival and social reasons for getting a good stink on.

A wolf would roll in the poo of his prey, thus masking his own scent. The hunter's quarry would not know it was in danger, instead thinking it was being tailed by a stinky member of its own species. Lured into a false sense of security, the animal would not flee and could be quickly devoured. This saved the wolf a lot of running around.

Status in the pack could also be elevated if a wolf had a knack for making impressive discoveries. He would announce these to the gang by covering himself in the odour of his finds. Even today, who wouldn't want to line up behind the guy who knows how to score choice fish heads?

Now that our meals come from tins and bags, and our regular social circles consist of old beach towels named Binky and stuffed dogs from the fun fair, our practical need to perfume ourselves is limited. Yet the desire is still there.

For a dog wanting to get back to his roots, there really isn't anything quite so instinctually satisfying as getting oneself good and rank.

Here's a short guide to the best smells and where to find them:

Poo

Preferably damp, fresh. As this can be a strictly DIY affair, it's among the most popular stinks. If you live on or near a farm, go for the cow pats. They're particularly moist and clingy.

Vomit

Again, this can be of your own making but tends to be much more gratifying if discovered elsewhere. Human deposits can often be found on Saturday and Sunday mornings outside the pub, under the football stands or in the park.

Foul Smells Every Dog Should Roll in

CARCASSES

Best quality available on warm, humid days. You can occasionally strike lucky in the garden, but the best troves are usually found during a walk in the woods, on the side of the road or at the beach during low tide.

FOETID SWAMPS

A pungent combination of wetness and decay, these may also contain bonus carcasses. Usually found in woodlands, but may be as close as the garden if your owner is lazy and can't be bothered to clean the pond.

RUBBISH

A true potpourri of nasty odours, rubbish bags may contain anything from fuzzy lasagna to dirty nappies. Toppling over a bin after a hot holiday weekend produces the best bounty.

EGGS

Typically found in rubbish, but the best opportunities tend to be seasonal. The park the week after an Easter egg roll and the neighbourhood pavements the morning after Halloween are particularly fertile grounds.

Literature

❖

Books are not easy to digest. They are often thick and hard to tear into, and without fail the ones that are really, really soft leave a bad taste in your mouth. In general they are hard work. Owners keep them around mostly to make visitors think they're clever and don't watch a lot of television.

Books can be about practically anything. Chances are that somewhere in your owner's library there is one about his favourite subject, which could very well be dogs, unless you were given to him as a last-minute surprise birthday gift.

Dog-training books sell but are generally pretty stupid. Often they are simply manuals listing insane prescriptions to either get you to stop, or start, doing something. As if you were going to cease barking at clouds or begin to leave the toilet paper alone simply because some trainer decided to write a book. All owners who buy books like this eventually find out that what might have worked for Mr Trainer won't necessarily work on you. Dog trainers are far better at training humans to buy their books and DVDs.

Dog fiction is also very popular. As a genre it owes a collective debt to one great man.

Jack London (long time ago – long time ago) was an American writer with an alcohol drinking problem and a way with words. He wrote two books about dogs that are considered by many to be the starting and ending points for literature featuring a canine protagonist.

The Call of the Wild is a book that every dog should know. Next time you are at the groomers, take a look and see if it's sitting with any of the glossy magazines that set impossible body-type and weight standards for young dogs. It's doubtful that it will be.

The Call of the Wild is a story about a pampered, fussed-over lump of a dog named Buck who gets kidnapped and taken to Alaska, where he has to work out in a hurry how to survive in a harsh, even primordial environment. Eventually Buck avenges the death of his final and kindly owner by killing a tribe of Indians. He then becomes the Alpha male of a wolf pack he meets upon his return to the wild.

White Fang is the companion to *The Call of the Wild* and has a reverse storyline. Instead of a domesticated dog being kidnapped and taken into the wild, White Fang concerns a captured wild dog taken to live with owners. White Fang saves his owner from a killer at the end. In those two ways it is different from *The Call of the Wild*.

Both books do an excellent job, through a realistic narrative, of providing perspective on what it is like to be a dog. They do not overly romanticize the sometimes harsh and cruel lives of Buck and White Fang, while reminding the reader of our full potential, both as dogs and as companions. For that, Jack London is a friend to dogs everywhere.

Following *The Call of the Wild*, *White Fang* and several other books that didn't sell as well, London died, young and exhausted.

Constellations

❖

They show up each night outside in the sky, which is the place high above our ears. Flickering little lights.

Some nights you can see them better than others, but every night they're up there. Sadly, many city dogs rarely get a glimpse; they don't get the opportunity to be outside at night. But country dogs have always observed the heavenly lights and pondered their existence.

Our ancestors believed that they were caused by the torches of animal control agents, or what used to be called dog catchers, roaming the skies. This notion caused many dogs to be frozen in fear at night, terrified the lights were coming for them.

Later, dogs often suffered unnecessary scoldings because they felt compelled to bark at the lights for as long as they could, believing they emanated from the torches of their owners. They felt confused and frustrated when the owners came running from the house, yelling 'Shut up!' instead of dropping from the sky.

We now know that both explanations are incorrect.

You probably wouldn't guess, it but much of the dark sky is actually food, toys and treats. Seem impossible? Take a look at this view of one group of lights:

That's what you probably see. They look moderately interesting but not really anything to get your tail wagging. Look a little closer, however, and you'll see something entirely different.

Bonius Minor

Now *there's* something to get us all licking our chops, and that's really just the beginning. It's like a wide-open refrigerator or a trip to the pet food emporium up there. Let's consider another example.

Yawn.

Beefus Major

Yum is more like it!

You're probably saying, 'Enough teasing. How do we get this stuff?' Well, the simple answer is that we can't; not yet, anyway. Someday we will probably be able to jump that high, but for now we're just going to have to be satisfied with knowing it's there.

The good news is that one of us is high above, guarding everything.

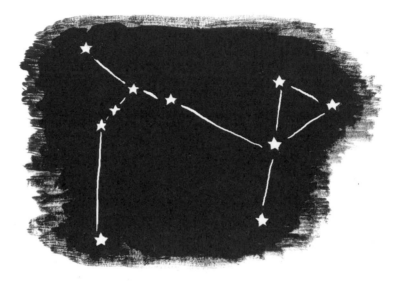

Canis Major

Nobody is really sure what breed Canis is. All that is known for certain is he's the biggest dog of them all. His collar contains the brightest light in the sky and can be seen best when he rises in the east during late summer. Don't ever bark at him, though, or he might decide to just help himself.

At last count there were more delicious and fun things up there than there are numbers. Next time you're outside at night, take a nice long look up and see if you can discover some new stuff. Who knows? You might be the one to find the package of hamburger nobody else knows about.

Courageous Dogs in History – Part Two

BELLE THE BEAGLE: Real-life Lifesaver

There's a reason most of us haven't been taught how to use the phone. Deep down, we know we would use it for all the wrong reasons: prank calls to the vet, long-distance howling, ordering four sausage pizzas with extra sausage. Belle the Beagle isn't like most of us. Her owner, a diabetic man from Florida, taught her to dial the phone if he ever passed out or suddenly became sick due to his condition and couldn't call for help.

Belle the Beagle

When her owner fell down and became unconscious, Belle did not call the restaurant, ask them if their refrigerator was running, and tell them that they had better go and chase it. She did not call her favourite radio station and try to win two tickets to see Toto. And although it was very tempting, she did not dial out for a Chinese takeway. She did exactly as she was trained to do and used her teeth to press the number '9' on the keypad. The '9' was preprogrammed to dial 911, and when the operators heard Belle's bark on the other end of the line they knew to rush an ambulance to the house. The paramedics arrived in time to save Belle's owner, which made Belle one happy Beagle. If that wasn't enough, she also won an award,which is like a very important treat, got her picture in all the papers, and dogs all over the country got a role model who would never be kicked off the couch again.

LOU – a bloody good dog

Lou didn't set out to be a hero. The four-year-old Border Collie had a reputation as a tough guy – a former rescue pup who only looked out for number one. So it wasn't that strange when, one crisp September morning, Lou stowed away on a rural school bus. It was against the rules, but Lou didn't care much for rules. He was bored. He was looking for adventure. And he knew exactly where to find it – aboard a rural school bus.

Sure enough, the school bus was a thrill, and the kids were a hoot. But just as Lou finished wolfing down the contents of three packed lunches there was suddenly a terrible noise and a big bump in the road.

Lou looked up and didn't like what he saw: old Bill Merrihue, the driver, slumped over the wheel! He'd been in enough cars to know that wasn't good. The bus was swerving wildly. The kids were screaming and crying. There was only one thing to do, and Lou knew he would have to be the one to do it.

Without wasting another second, he scampered to the driver's seat, jumped on old Merrihue's lap and deftly steered the careening school bus back onto the road. A giant cheer erupted as the bus steadied safely on the road. Naturally, everyone who saw the incident was very surprised. None of them knew Lou could drive a manual transmission.

All seemed well again, but as Lou eyed a bridge up ahead, he knew he had another big problem on his paws. A large chunk of the bridge was missing.

Lou didn't know much, but he knew a thing or two about bridges. One of the two things Lou knew about bridges was that they were easier to drive across than water. The other thing he knew was that they didn't work if they had giant holes in them. Lou had to make a difficult choice – either stop the bus and wait for help, or step on the accelerator and jump the bridge. He didn't know what would happen if he hit the accelerator, but he knew what would happen to old Merrihue if he didn't. That wasn't a chance Lou was prepared to take.

Lou steeled his nerves, pushed his paw to the pedal and the pedal to the metal, and held his breath. He also closed his eyes and whimpered a little, but he wouldn't want anybody to know that. The bus sailed over the bridge like a Frisbee in the park on Sunday, and touched down gently on the other side. Everyone on the school bus breathed a big sigh of relief which sounded a little bit like this: 'AHHHHHHHHHHH-HHH'.

Lou dropped old Merrihue off at the hospital, and waited around to make sure he would be OK. Then he got back in the bus, drove it right past the school without even slowing down, and steered it straight to Pronto Pizza, where he bought margaritas for all the kids on board – every one.

And that's exactly how it happened.

Courageous Dogs in History – Part Two

How to Choose and
Bury a Bone

—————— ❖ ——————

Bones are wonderful, and great to chew on for hours at a time. The only problem is that the dog is usually finished before the bone is. What can you do with a bone in between hearty chewing sessions? The answer is right under your feet, at least it is if you are outside. Ages ago, dogs used to bury excess food in order to keep it safe from scavengers. While bones are not food, they go in your mouth, exactly where food goes, and they taste great, just like food. In order to keep them safe from other dogs or owners who want to clean up, and to help them retain their flavour, left-over bones should be buried so you can come back and retrieve them at your leisure.

On the surface, burying a bone appears to be a simple, straightforward task. After all, digging holes is innate to dogs. This is deceptive. Most dogs aren't given the proper amount of private outdoor time needed to bury bones in secrecy. Furthermore, most owners are very uptight about having holes dug in the garden. They always forget that it is your garden. You spend more time in it. You poo there. You don't tell them what to do in their bedrooms, do you? Don't let them tell you what to do in your garden.

You will need:

1. a bone
2. a spot of soft earth

Choosing the right bone is a matter of canine preference. For the purposes of this discussion, a bone is any item with chewing value, whether or not it is derived from an animal's skeleton. Bones can be broken down into two categories: natural and synthetic.

NATURAL

Most bones are cow- or pig-based, but don't close yourself off to surprises. Dogs in Scotland north enjoy the occasional bone made from deer, and our Australian Cattle Dog friends sing the praises of kangaroo bones. Bones in the 'natural' category include real bones, cow and pig hooves, and rawhide and pigs' ears. All natural bones tend to become very sticky once you get saliva on them! This makes them more fun to lick and gnaw and less attractive for owners who want to take them away from you.

TYPE	ADVANTAGES	DISADVANTAGES
Pork or beef bone	Delicious, tough, can last for days	Hard to come by
Hooves	Stink like crazy	May give you the runs
Rawhide/pigs' ears	Fit in mouth perfectly, hard for owners to prise out of mouth	Can make your tummy hurt, may carry disease
Chicken bones	Quite tasty	Dangerous – can get lodged in your throat and hurt an awful lot

SYNTHETIC

Synthetic, or fake, bones are made by humans as a substitute for the real thing. Your instincts are not wrong. This is weird. Look around. Almost everything that walks is full of bones. With all these bones walking around everywhere, you would think that there would be an abundance of bones that they would want to get rid of. This does not seem to be the case.

How to Choose and Bury a Bone

Many synthetics are designed to clean your teeth. This is evil. They steal away valuable food remnants lodged on your teeth that could be used for later snacking. In any event, this does not make them any less fun to chew on and growl over. Some say fake bones are harder to destroy. This is your challenge. Who is the boss, you or some fake bone? When it comes to burying synthetic bones, use caution. They smell much less than natural bones and are therefore not ideal for burying, as you might not be able to find them later.

TYPE	ADVANTAGES	DISADVANTAGES
Plastic bones	Tough, chewy	Odourless and tasteless
Rubber bones	May last for hours	Shape and texture make them too easy for owners to remove from mouths
Plush bones	May harbour squeakers	Hardly a bone at all

BURYING YOUR BONE

Once you've chosen and savoured your bone, you may now bury it. Give yourself ample time to do it right. Pretend you have to pee so you will be let outside. In fact, once you're out, it's probably a good idea to pee anyway. Don't dawdle, though.

Scout out the garden. Look for a good out-of-the way space where you will not be spotted. A corner is good, but not if there's a tree there. It is very difficult to dig around roots. Bare earth is the best, but you can dig through grass if need be.

Stay away from flower beds. While they have a lot of open, inviting soil and are very easy to dig up, a missing flower is like a sign saying 'THERE IS A BONE HERE.' You're trying to *hide* your bone, not tell every-

No   *Yes*

one where it is. Also, your owners have an odd attachment to any plants you need to get rid of in order to dig. If you get caught, it's very likely that you will be stopped in mid-dig and your bone will be taken away. Garden privileges may be suspended for a time as well.

Now that you've found your spot, start digging. Use your forepaws, use your snout, just kick that earth! You will know when you have finished if there is a hole where earth used to be. Place your bone in the hole and cover it up, quick! Now, look around. Make sure you remember the scent of your bone and where you buried it so you can dig it up again later.

Most importantly, never bury your bone in a cemetery. The bone smell is overwhelming, and you might not be able to find yours. And if you think owners get angry when you dig a hole in their garden, just wait till they see you with a cemetery bone.

THE CITY DOG ALTERNATIVE

Sadly, if you are a city dog without a garden, the likelihood that you will be able to get to a burying spot is poor. Instead, knock your bones under a couch or another hard-to-reach spot when you've finished with it. You won't be able to retrieve them at your leisure, but when your owner cleans the room, you'll have a treasure-trove of half-chewed bones to choose from!

Squirrels

———————— ❖ ————————

It's hard to articulate exactly what is so annoying about squirrels. They don't really do us or our owners any harm, but at the same time they're always around! Argh! Soooo annoying! Whenever you want to play fetch, they're in the way. They're always running around our gardens without asking first. Want to beg for scraps at an outdoor picnic? Chances are you'll have competition from some obnoxious little grey rodent. The worst part of all this is that many owners actually think these squirrels are adorable.

We've tried to be friendly neighbours and set some basic boundaries. We've told them time and again that as long as they keep their infuriating zipping, digging and running up and down trees out of our view, we won't have a problem. But there comes a point when diplomacy is fruitless and you've got to take action.

Though squirrels look harmless, remember that there is a reason why a species like the black and red bush squirrel, commonly found in Malawi, Tanzania and Zambia, has the Latin name *Paraxerus lucifer*. They're devilish. If you remain passive, eventually their constant needling becomes more than a mere nuisance. They'll honestly start to believe they have free rein over your garden.

Squirrels are found all over the world and come in more than 360 varieties – all of which are getting a bit too big for their boots. Here is a guide to a few of these species and some useful information on how to get them to stop annoying the life out of you.

COMMON SPECIES

The *Fox Squirrel* is one of the most common types of the pest in North America. They are a particular problem for most American dogs since they spend more time on public grounds than any other tree squirrel. A

particularly annoying trait of theirs is how they flaunt their enormous tails. Their breeding seasons are in December and June, so this would be an ideal time to delicately suggest that they spend lots of time hidden from view. Start barking as if you have spotted some of their natural enemies (e.g. hawks, snakes, bobcats, a few creepy humans). That should send them running.

Fox Squirrel

Western and **Eastern Grey Squirrels** are dim-witted creatures who suffer from a serious lack of common courtesy. They are two of the largest species in North America and spend their entire morning foraging for food in our gardens – treating them like they're a big public refrigerator. Greys have no qualms about going so far as to set up nests in attics or even within the very walls of our owners' homes. They steal birdseed from our bird feeders at will, and, as a true testament to their inconsiderate ways, they have crossed the ocean (presumably by using the water-skiing skills they have learned at roadside petting zoos and animal circuses) and have spread across the United Kingdom, Italy and South Africa. As dogs, we must protect our homes and homelands from the greys. Scouring our gardens for chestnuts is one thing, but entering our homes is a bold display of impropriety that must be dealt with swiftly.

Grey squirrel

Squirrels

American Red Squirrels and **Douglas Squirrels** are essentially the same obnoxious creature. They are known collectively as 'pine squirrels' because they have centred their diet on the seeds of conifer trees. If you live in an area rich in pine and cedar trees, you will have to bear the brunt of these species' adolescent antics. The red's and the Douglas's short lifespan of 1–3 years is a bit deceptive. You might not bother to banish them, thinking they won't be around for long, but they breed with such gusto that it's important to keep after them. No dog likes to lie, but these beasts are so oversexed that spreading a rumour about ovulating females hiding at the bottom of a lake might quickly take care of your problem.

American Red and Douglas Squirrel

Japanese Giant Flying Squirrel

Dogs of Japan, we do not envy you. The giant flying squirrel is around 45 cm long (so it's giant in offensiveness, not size) and can glide from tree to tree. A squirrel hurling insults from a treetop is pretty annoying, but it's even more annoying coming from a squirrel soaring overhead.

Japanese Giant Flying Squirrel

Squirrels

European Souslik

From the Ukraine to the Czech Republic to Poland and all the way down to Greece, this nettlesome being stuffs seeds, roots and insects into its gullet every summer. There's nothing quite so annoying as spending all day begging for a cheese dumpling only to see it plucked away by a souslik. Luckily, we only have to deal with them during the hot months, before they scurry underground for their extended hibernation period. Chasing them out of a garden should be fairly effortless, since they are especially tubby and slow during their feeding period, but whatever you do, don't get on the bad side of the colony's sentinel or it'll never stop whistling the most irritating warning call you've ever heard.

European Souslik

What to Do During
a Thunderstorm

The Scram and Cower method was first created by the Canine Defence Council in cooperation with the National Hiding Association as a simple and easy-to-remember way to protect yourself during a thunderstorm attack.

First, it's important for you to know what a thunderstorm is and what it can do to you.

We share a tense, delicate coexistence with nature. Like a cat, nature is easily annoyed. It can be provoked by seemingly minor infractions such as eating a specific blade of grass or digging up a mostly dead hydrangea. But nature has something much more frightening than a paw full of sharp claws at its disposal. Nature has the ability to unleash a mighty thunderstorm.

A thunderstorm can harm you in many ways. The water nature sends down from the clouds can make your fur disappear. The winds it brings will try to steal the bark right out of your mouth. Its bolts of light can freeze you in an unflattering position. If caught outside in a thunderstorm you could be destroyed, or at least permanently embarrassed.

A thunderstorm attack can come with very little warning, so a smart dog should always be alert and well prepared. A smart dog knows how to Scram and Cower!

Even on the most magnificent of afternoons, you should always be on the look-out for signs. The heavens can quickly darken and the air becomes prickly. You may hear a rumble, like a pack of Dobermans galloping across the clouds. The sky will flicker, as if its light switch is malfunctioning. And the trees, having a direct line to nature, will become worked up, swaying to and fro.

If you notice any of those things, get inside or find cover elsewhere, and do it as quickly as you can! Scram and Cower!

Once a thunderstorm hits, there will be terrific bursts of light, brighter than the noon sky and brighter than a thousand camera flashbulbs. They will be followed by a hideous, ear-splitting roar, a sound more terrifying than when your owner spilled a coffee and burned his hand.

You must Scram and Cower!

First, make sure you've already chosen and stocked your designated safe zones. In the wardrobe and under the bed are ideal choices. These often afford additional levels of protection, such as your owner's abandoned gym clothes or old copies of the *Radio Times*.

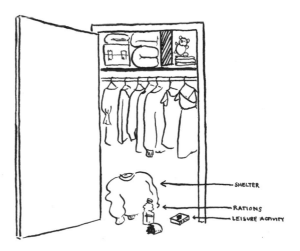

SHELTER

RATIONS
LEISURE ACTIVITY

What to Do During a Thunderstorm

In the event your designated safe zones are not immediately accessible during an attack, you should climb behind or beneath anything close by; just be sure you are adequately covered. Wedge yourself behind the fridge or pull the hall carpet up with your teeth and worm under it. Scram and Cower!

If you cannot get inside when a thunderstorm strikes, find protection wherever you can. Under the barbecue cover or beneath the trampoline in the neighbour's garden – these places will give you adequate protection until the danger's over. Scram and Cower!

Know that once you Scram and Cower a thunderstorm cannot hurt you. You are safe and should stay where you are until your owner assures you that everything is all right.

Remember, a prepared dog is a safe dog. Make sure you know where your safe zones are. Make sure you know where you can go when you're not close to your safe zones. And remember, when you see that flash – what do you do? That's right. Scram and Cower!

Epic Walks – Part Two
The Argo

———— ❖ ————

The following tale has never been written down before, but it is most certainly familiar to you since it has been passed down through barking tradition for centuries. This is the story of Argos, loyal dog to the man of many turns, Odysseus. While Odysseus traipsed around the sea for twenty philandering-filled years, Argos stayed on land and had an adventure of his own. Here is the First Book of the classic Greek epic poem, *The Argo.*

ARGO, I

Bark, O Howler –

Of the sturdy hound,
The walker, of great distance and true speed
Following abandonment by his Master.

Bark
Of all the lands he marked, the bitches humped,
The anguish in his breast and deep panting
While battling to retrieve and to lead his pack
Who would not heed his growls –
Yapping mutts – put down by their own appetites
When they scoffed the Siren's juicy steak,
And that T-bone did undo their mortal collar.

Of these times,
Bark, Eternal Howler,
And wail the story for our perked ears.

Now, with Master Odysseus at sea –
Gentle Penelope commands Loyal Argos –
She balks at suitor after suitor, ordering her hound
And his pack to bite the ankles and hides
Of the bearded men who trouble her.
Though he remains obedient, Argos stares,
Puppy-eyed, at his lady. A quest of many strides
He begs for—
                    With tail wagging.

Young Telemachus, boy-man of Master Odysseus,
Observes his furry, four-legged brother –
The thirst to chase bonds the disparate species,
And with a mighty pull of his bow
The Human Child releases a soaring toy into the sky.

As hazy fingers of dawn bathe the airborne plaything,
The gods gather upon Mt Canis –
Thundering Rover bellows in the Great Kennel:

'Canines! They yelp for playtime, but for their fun
They do not repay with ample poo!
This Argos allows his Masters to pick up his turds,
Leaving none on the ground as a sacrifice to his gods!
For his affront, let him never find the toy
His Young Telemachus has thrown!'

Wise goddess Betsy pierces Rover with her Greyhound eyes:

'True, O noble Rover, whose snarl can bring about
Piddle in even the largest mortal Mastiff –
But remember our Argos is a most good dog.
He, who has buried the largest bone,
He, who has treed the foulest squirrel,
He, who has honoured his gods with strong breeding.
Test him if you must, but an endless chase
              Is too severe.'

Rover, Father of Dogs, listened to Grey-Furred Betsy,
His rage cooled by her delicate barks.

'So it will be. Let the woods grow dense
Around the fallen toy –
              But Loyal Argos
Shall not have his beloved game of chase lead
Him forever away from home.'

              So swift-footed Argos
Began his pursuit of the toy,
Though the day of chase would soon turn dark.

Riding in a Car

First there's the feel of the breeze blowing your fur. Then there's the chance to pant or bark at dozens of strangers. Your tail wags excitedly as the smells of the world waft by you like a runaway buffet table. Sound too good to be true? Well you're not dreaming – you're in a car!

A ride in a car is an adventure like no other. Jump in one, and you never know where you'll end up. You might be going to friend's house, the pet shop, or even the fancy dog park. Who knows? What's certain is that you're going, and you'll get there a lot faster than walking.

Rides are a thrill, no matter what kind of dog you are. Big dog? Romp around the cab of your owner's lorry, stick your head out the window and bark up a storm – you're the toughest cur alive! Little dog? Ride in the front with your owner, put your paws on the steering wheel and smile! You're the captain of the ship!

Nearly every dog remembers his first car ride. Many of us were reluctant puppies in crates who didn't even know what wheels were. But gradually we learned not to be afraid. Why, just look out the window! There's a whole world rolling by. Does it get any better? It does! Because here's the best part: Almost every trip promises a return trip. So if you ride there, you also ride back. That's two rides, every time. Every time!

A WARNING ABOUT CARS: Cars are wonderful and promise something new every day. But sometimes they don't take us to the park. Sometimes they take us to the boarding kennel. Sometimes, to the vet. Many of us have been lured into a car with the promise of a ride, only to wake up with our balls missing. Where did they go? Can we ever get them back? Sadly, few of us will ever know.

It's understandable that you might be a little wary about going for a ride. Don't be. These things do happen, but life is nothing without risk – and a ride in a car on a beautiful day is worth just about any risk.

GOING!

If your owner is swearing while he looks for his keys, wallet and mobile phone, it is a good indicator that he is taking the car. Now that you know you're going, how do you know where you're going? This is hard, as cars can take people and dogs practically anywhere on earth. Luckily, with a little know-how, you can usually work it out. Here are a few clues as to where you might be going:

The Park

Look for the lead. It's a dead giveaway. If you're really lucky, your owner is wearing sports clothes. But that doesn't happen very often.

Errands

Owners are always doing something they call 'running errands'. These aren't much fun, since you usually have to stay in the car with the window rolled down while they get petrol or wait in line at the post office, and you don't get the chance to do much running. But it beats being stuck at home with the squeezy toy and another episode of *Emmerdale*.

Holiday

Is your bowl coming? How about your blanket and a bag of dry food? Get ready, boy – you might be going on a road trip!

RULES OF THE ROAD

Cars stop and start a lot, and they also go fast and slow, so be prepared. You have to obey your owner, but in a car your owner has to obey something too. They're called the rules of the road. Here's how it works:

Traffic Lights

These tell people what to do.

The grey light on top means 'stay'.

The grey light on the bottom means 'come'.

The grey one in the middle means 'speed up and use the horn'.

Stop Sign

This is a funny-shaped sign that says something. It means slow the car down, but don't stop, and then speed up again. Something like that.

Finally, is the driver next to your owner handsome or pretty? If you can get this person to look at your owner and tell them how cute you are, you will definitely get a treat.

HOW TO CONDUCT YOURSELF IN A CAR

We're all excited beyond our wildest dreams to be in a car. If you act up too much, though, you risk losing the opportunity to ride in a car again. Nobody, least of all you, wants to see that happen. Here are some simple rules for canine conduct in and around cars:

- If you are asked 'Do you want to go for a ride?' you should always respond with an affirmative bark. Don't hum, don't haw, don't hesitate, just bark 'yes'.
- Whenever possible hang your head out of the window – mouth open, tongue hanging out all the way. This maximizes your joy as well as that of your owner, making future car trips more likely.
- Make eye contact with passengers in other cars. This lets them know how much you are enjoying yourself, and how much more they would be enjoying themselves if they had a dog in their car. It's just good politics.
- Although it may be tempting, remember to never get too worked up in a car. Loud barking could startle your owner, who is already nervous because of that man in the uniform driving behind you.
- Lastly, no matter where you go, be sure to smile. After all – you're in a car!

Dog Jobs

----------------- ❖ -----------------

There was a time when we dogs were expected to earn our keep. We were proud to work for our supper – guarding the hearth, leading the hunt, sinking our teeth into the juicy calves of our owners' enemies. It helped us bond with our humans, gave us plenty of good exercise, and filled us with a sense of pride and purpose.

Nowadays, instead of actually earning a living, most of us just sit around, idle-pawed and out of work. Thankfully, there will always be a few jobs just for dogs. We don't care how intelligent it is – no dolphin or cat is going to protect your owner's home.

Of course, your full-time job is being man's best friend – but there's no reason you can't have a rewarding career outside the home. Here are a few jobs you might be suited for.

ASSISTANCE DOGS

Are you a bright, duty-bound puppy? Become an assistance dog. You get to go to special schools, wear a smart harness and help people do all sorts of things. Best of all, you're allowed to go to places the rest of us aren't, like all the best-smelling restaurants and grocers, and on tours of sausage-making facili-ties during Oktoberfest. Assistance dogs are usually Labradors or Retrievers, but any good, clean-cut, level-headed puppy can try out and see if he's got the right stuff. People may not pet you as much, but they'll respect you. And your owner will be proud.

GUARD DOGS

Traditionally the domain of Doberman Pinschers, Rottweilers and Pit Bulls, the work of a guard dog is never done, and one has to be ready to attack at any moment. This is a high-stress job, but it has its perks. Employers will reward you with treats and affection for keeping the place safe, and thieves will try to bribe you with nice, juicy steaks that they keep in their pockets. Taking the bribe is not really ethical, but maybe you can work out a way to play both ends of the pitch. Totally up to you.

SCRAPYARD DOGS

Are you a surly, barky sort with a bad attitude? Do you enjoy lying around all day, sleeping in a shed, and making a racket all night long? Do you enjoy chewing on tractor tyres and scaring the bejeezus out of people? Then this job is for you. The pay isn't great, but you're pretty much your own boss and make your own hours. Besides, who else is going to employ a vicious maniac like you?

HERDERS

There are many different types of herders. Some are trained specifically to herd cattle and pigs, but the most popular kind is probably the Sheepdog. Regardless of his lineage, there's no reason any self-respecting mutt can't keep a couple of sheep in line. After all, they're sheep. They do what they're told. How hard can it be?

Being a sheperd is a great chance to enjoy the out-of-doors, all day, every day. Of course, you have to put up with all that bleating, but it's worth it when you get to scare off the occasional predator.

FIRESTATION DOGS

These working dogs are really popular in the U.S. It's traditionally a Dalmatian-run business, but opportunities have been popping up for the rest of us these last few years. The downside is that you're always on call and you may have to run into a burning building, or pose for a calendar with a bunch of shirtless firefighters. The upside? A job in a fire station is like a one-way ticket to Burger Town. These guys love to eat. All the cooking is done on the premises. And everybody loves a firestation dog. Yup, firestation dogs have got it made.

DRUG AND BOMB SNIFFING DOGS

If you love action, adventure and sniffing, this is the job for you. You ride around in special cars and hang out at airports, where you will meet some very, very nervous university students. Sometimes you even wear a special vest, and unlike other vests this one makes you look tough.

These guys are the elite guard, dogdom's finest. Joining the force isn't for everybody, but for dogs dedicated to justice and honour, and pooches who live to serve and protect, it's the only life there is. Pay attention and keep your nose to the ground, and some day you might even make it to detective.

SEARCH-AND-RESCUE DOGS

If danger is your middle name, look no further. As a search-and-rescue dog, you'll travel wherever there's trouble and wherever people need help. Avalanche in the mountains? You're the one locating survivors and helping pull them to safety. Hikers lost in the woods? You're the one who finds them and gets all the hugs. You're helping flood victims one day, and reuniting a little lost girl with her parents the next. The perks? Joyful reunions that would never have happened without you and your snout, and all the glory you can handle. This job is great for playful dogs with a keen sense of smell and a true nose for daring.

SECRETARY GENERAL
OF THE UNITED NATIONS

Are you exceedingly diplomatic? Do you enjoy political manoeuvring, effective negotiations, sharing your biscuits, and international relations? If so, this is the job for you. As Secretary General of the United Nations you have to be fair, just and willing to stand up for the interests of others, all while your conduct is being held up to constant scrutiny. It's a tough but truly rewarding job that can help you change the world, and only selfless, loyal dogs need apply.

What's Edible?

———— ❖ ————

We all know that just about everything our owners put in our food bowls is great to eat. But what about everything else?

Well, that depends on you. A dog's palate is generally determined by three factors: age, breed and hunger level. A moderately snacky Husky puppy might turn a room of linoleum flooring into his own personal hall of pork scratchings, while an adult Husky with that same level of hunger might wait for a while until he finds a crisp. An Alsatian may give an off-season crab cake a miss, whereas a Poodle would probably snatch it up even after eating his own weight in ham.

Whoever put this world together made sure our lives were filled with dizzying opportunities to slurp something up and give it a whirl around the taste buds. Or at least chew it up really well and hide it under the couch.

Whatever your taste, you'll always find something that seems as though it should be eaten. But just because something is *potentially* edible doesn't necessarily mean it's *advisably* edible. There isn't a dog out there who doesn't have a sad tale of eater's remorse to share, so to help you get the good stuff and avoid a trip to the V-E-T, we've put together a short primer on some frequently ingested items.

KEY TO EDIBILITY

🐾 🐾 🐾 🐾 🐾 **Top shelf!**

🐾 🐾 🐾 🐾 **Outstanding nosh**

🐾 🐾 🐾 **Pretty tasty, but with reservations**

🐾 🐾 **For the daring eater only**

🐾 **If you absolutely must**

🐾 **Blech! And/or Ouch!**

VOMIT/POO

🐾🐾🐾🐾🐾

Your front and back ends are basically around-the-clock delis, dispensing convenient and renewable munchies. If you were really enthusiastic about that two-week-old Polish sausage but it didn't sit well with your stomach the first time, this is like winning a second chance.

BUBBLEGUM

🐾🐾🐾🐾

Bubblegum is a great snack for the dog on the go. Found on pavements everywhere, it comes in hard, sticky and gravelly varieties and in an assortment of flavours. Humans love the sight of a dog chewing bubblegum, so if you find some, chew it vigorously. Someone might take your picture!

PILLOWS

🐾🐾🐾

Tearing through the exterior of a pillow can be difficult and wearing on the jaw, but if you've got the stamina, a wonderful surprise awaits – mountains of foam or goose feathers! You can track the pillow guts all over the house and stash them in your hiding place for later. Pillows reach their peak deliciousness when your owner goes away.

KEYS

♣

Some dogs are always up for an eating challenge, and these shiny, jangly sticks certainly are one. We don't like to hold anyone back, but be warned. They're hard going in and even harder coming out. And if you happen to swallow the one set that makes the car go, forget rides for a while.

MOBILE PHONES

♣ ♣

Mobile phones might seem as though they've got a good flavour since your owner always has one by his mouth, but they're really just hard and taste like ear. The antenna is good to chew on for a while, but ultimately these just break into sharp pieces and are really not worth the effort. Also, without one, your owner won't be willing to take you out as much because he has to 'wait for calls'.

BELTS

♣ ♣ ♣ ♣

Belts are like heavenly rawhide that goes on forever. Despite being pretty attached to these delicacies, our owners often leave them lying around for us to find. If you bag one, expect to be punished for a little while, but not too long. Humans grow belts back pretty quickly.

ROCKS

You may mistake rocks for stray bits of hamburger. When you get one in your mouth, you instantly know it's not hamburger, but you might continue to chew on it hoping that maybe there's hamburger inside. This will just leave you disappointed and angry. Sometimes with fewer teeth.

IMPORTANT PAPERS

Once a piece of paper has handwriting on it, that piece of paper transforms into an inky treat. Emergency phone numbers, complex maths problems, song lyrics, scientific discoveries and lists of computer passwords all have unique flavours you won't get from any old blank piece of paper. Sometimes these fight back and cut your tongue, so give them a good slobbering first.

WARNING! There are a few things that, while deceptively tasty, could make you extremely ill and quite possibly kill you. Under no circumstances should you ever consider putting any of the following in your mouth:

- lilies, azaleas and many other plants (for safety's sake, just leave the plants alone)
- chocolate
- onions and garlic
- macadamia nuts.

Scavenge widely, scoff wisely!

Territory – What It Is, Why It's Yours and Why You Must Defend It at All Costs

❖

Territory is all the land that a canine considers to be his natural domain. Sometimes it's called 'property', 'terrain', or 'turf', but no matter what you call it, it belongs to you.

After all, you've earned it. You've worked hard and put up with a lot to get where you are today. You've torn up countless flower beds and a good deal of costly porch furniture to get the garden exactly how you want it. The last thing you need is some postman beating his own path to the doorstep, getting goodness knows whose scent on everything you've sprayed. This is your *owner's house* we're talking about, and what's his is yours. Except for the mortgage payments. Those are all his.

If you've ever eaten a map, you may have noticed that human territories have boundaries. Yours do too. Boundaries are important, but as you've noticed, cats, birds and parcel carriers will not respect them. Squirrels, foxes, and even other dogs will also try to encroach upon your established turf. You turn your back on a frisky scamp for one minute – the next thing you know he's sucking up to YOUR owner and eating YOUR food out of YOUR bowl. In YOUR house. That's just the kind of thing that happens if you let your guard down. Don't.

The bottom line is, you don't just have a right to protect what's yours, you've got a *duty* to protect what's yours, and the instinct to do so is at the very heart of what makes you a dog. It is a fact of life that you will have to defend your territory and possessions (bones, toys, food bowls) against intruders frequently. Do so swiftly and forcefully.

There is a common misconception among our owners that our territory extends to the foot of their property and not an inch further. Nothing could be further from the truth.

Your territory extends far beyond your garden, and you can expand it at virtually any time. Got your eye on a shady walnut tree? Sniff it out. If it hasn't been marked, just lift your leg and it belongs to you. Thinking about putting a second kennel out in front of the nail bar? Go for it! Once you start to look at the world in this way, you'll see that there's no limit to the number of property opportunities out there. Remember, anything you can pee on can be yours, if you are willing to defend it. It's squatting at its finest!

Of course, the more territory you acquire, the more you have to defend. It can be difficult to keep track of everything that's yours. The following diagram will help you determine if something is yours, and if you should race downstairs to defend it.

Territory – What It Is, Why It's Yours and Why You Must Defend It at All Costs

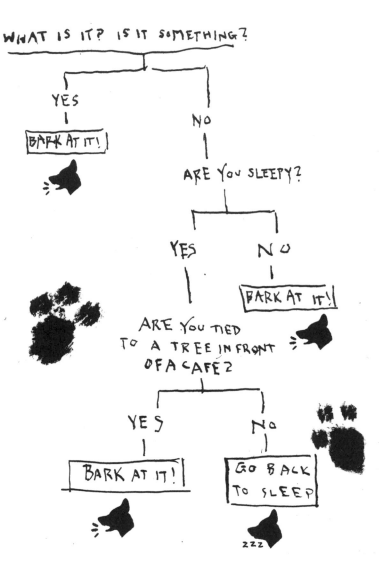

WHAT IS IT? IS IT SOMETHING?

YES — BARK AT IT!

NO — ARE YOU SLEEPY?

YES — ARE YOU TIED TO A TREE IN FRONT OF A CAFE?

NO — BARK AT IT!

YES — BARK AT IT!

NO — GO BACK TO SLEEP

Remember: Once you have decided that something belongs to you, you must defend it at all costs! This is of the utmost importance. Everything you've worked for is at stake. No trespass should be tolerated.

Territory – What It Is, Why It's Yours and Why You Must Defend It at All Costs

The Origin of Parks

—————— ❖ ——————

For many of us, parks are the only place we can really stretch our legs and sniff some prime tail. The thrice-daily walk on a lead is good for basic physical maintenance, but it's hard to break into a sprint when your chubby owner is weighing you down. The odd thing about the park is that while it allows for unfettered fun and was seemingly invented for canines, it was actually created as an excuse for humans to have the stupidest conversations imaginable.

HERE'S HOW IT HAPPENED

Around the year 7000 B.C. in the Mesopotamian region known as the Fertile Crescent, man began to develop a complex language system that nearly rivalled our own. What made our language superior, both then and now, is that it dispenses with semantics, minutiae and trivialities, whereas man-language appears to be entirely dependent on those characteristics.

As man-language grew, our owners wanted a forum to express their idiotic thoughts on history, politics, sports, science and love. The early marketplaces and shipping ports of Egypt, Greece and Rome turned out to be inappropriate venues for daft conversations. Every time a fishmonger or spice merchant tried to sell his goods, a buyer would stall the transaction by regaling all in earshot with some moronic story about

---

TIMELINE OF POINTLESS QUOTES FROM THE PARK

600 B.C., Olmec Empire, Southern Mexico: 'Man, I got a huge muscle cramp yesterday during the Mesoamerican football match. I'm going to have to make an appointment at the bloodletter or something.'

481 B.C., Iron Age Celtic civilization, England: 'Excuse me, do you know what time it is? Oh, I forgot, my dog is peeing on a gigantic stone clock. Never mind!'

---

taking his new boat for a spin in the Aegean Sea. The economy went nowhere amid the din. Humans needed a special area where their pointless drivel wouldn't interfere with commerce.

In 27 B.C., Man-Emperor Caesar Augustus ushered in the *Pax Romana*. Thanks to the new age of peace, stupid, vapid dialogues began to flourish now that the Romans weren't spending every single hour of the day trying to conquer the world. During this period, Augustus ordered hundreds of sculptures (mostly of himself) to be placed on the streets. These statues became natural meeting posts for dogs and humans alike, as they were easily identifiable landmarks, and very convenient to pee on. While dogs did their business on the sculptures, owners had the opportunity to engage in idle chatter. This fusion of excrement and mindless confabulation naturally laid the groundwork for the first parks. Soon, every human desperate for pathetically droll conversation was buying a dog so that he'd have an excuse to meet up at a Roman pee-pole.

Eventually, the people implored Augustus to build a proper park where dogs could run around for an extended period of time, enabling their owners to converse inanely for an equal – uninterrupted – period of time. He complied and in 9 B.C. erected the famous *Ara Pacis et Canis Ortus* (The Altar of Majestic Peace and Dog Park) on the Campus Martius along the river Tiber.

A TIMELINE OF POINTLESS QUOTES FROM THE PARK

- A.D. 409, Visigoth kingdom, Germany: 'I don't see why we should help Honorius, Emperor of the West, re gain control of the Iberian peninsula. It's his problem that he can't beat back the Vandal horde, not ours.'
- 467, Gupta empire, Northern India: 'Have you heard about this new number, zero? Very weird. It's no positive and it's not negative, so what on earth *is* it?'
- 869, Great Moravian empire, Slovakia: 'I can't seem to get used to that Cyrillic alphabet we're all sup posed to be using now. Every time I start to write a to-do list, I realize I'm using the wrong letters an have to start all over again.'

The Ara Pacis Park

Parks quickly spread throughout the Roman Empire as humans sought out more and more locations to gab ad nauseam about the poor performance of their local gladiators or about the latest melodrama from Seneca the Younger.

Though the Roman Empire eventually fell, the rise of the park continued, and in 1682 France's Louis XIV cut the ribbon on the most elaborate and magnificent park ever built: the Court of Versailles. It was here where Poodles frolicked freely among the ornate parterres, luxurious lawns, expansive canals and gorgeous fountains as courtiers and sycophants of the Sun King bandied about some of the most vapid, imbecilic and inconsequential babble ever uttered on earth.

The Park at Versailles

A TIMELINE OF POINTLESS QUOTES FROM THE PARK

1065, Norman kingdom, France: 'Do you think we should conquer England next year? I think I do. I don't know. My dad thinks we should.'

1181, Khmer empire, Cambodia: 'On paper, Jayavarman VII looks like a great king. I just hope he doesn't put his Mahayana Buddhism before the people.'

1225, Mongol empire, Eurasia: 'I know I should be drinking more yak milk, but it's so expensive. Five silver akçe for a single bottle? Do I look like Moneybags Khan?'

Today, parks have lost some of their ancient opulence, but they are no less fun to visit. Thankfully, an ever-expanding cable-channel line-up, gossip blogs, political scandals and an increase in the number of Premier League games have all ensured that owners still have plenty of asinine topics to prattle on about. Also, if your owner is single, you can probably bet you'll be going to the park at least four times a week. So the next time you hear some human jawing off to a stranger about how he's thinking of taking his speedboat out on the lake this weekend, just remember that it's that kind of gobbledygook that affords you the opportunity to run free for a half-hour.

A TIMELINE OF POINTLESS QUOTES FROM THE PARK

- 1603, Algonquin civilization, North America: 'Hey, those European birds who arrived the other day are hot with a capital H. I mean sizzling.'
- 1858, Zulu empire, South Africa: 'Yeah, I used to be really into the early Mbaqanga sound, but it's getting so commercial now. I've actually been listening to a lot of the old Maskanda classics lately.'

Sounds They Can't Hear

A dog's superior auditory sense is one of the things that sets us apart from owners and other human beings. Our keen ears pick up things they miss entirely.

To put a number on it, we hear with a sensitivity four times keener than theirs. That fact is obvious every day. You don't see their ears twitching when the lady across the street fires up her can opener, or when that squirrel in oak no. 5 moves up ten feet.

Not only are they unable to hear everything that may be trying to sneak up on them, they just aren't blessed like we are in the higher frequencies. Their ability to hear sounds stops at about 20,000 kHz, while ours goes beyond 50,000 kHz.

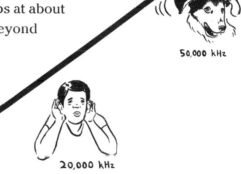

50,000 kHz

20,000 kHz

Due to this disparity in ability, there are times when we react to something that they can't hear. Some kind of unfortunate scolding situation usually ensues.

Didn't they learn anything from that part in *Superman, the Movie* where Gene Hackman broadcasts a message on a frequency that only Superman and dogs could hear? Dogs all over the planet heard it and barked like mad. That's what it's like sometimes. You just can't help yourself. If owners could be tuned in like we are, they would never scold us for barking again. Not only would they understand our reaction, but they'd probably be amazed at how bland their own auditory world really is.

Owners think they're doing you some kind of big favour by leaving the radio on, but they're not. Any dog who has been stuck at home all day with the radio while his owner was away knows it can be downright torturous, especially in the morning. If that one bloke laughing constantly isn't driving you to stick your head between the sofa cushions, then you're dunking it in the toilet every ten minutes because the monotone voices on Radio 4 make you sleepy.

Someday maybe we'll get our own radio station. We all know there's plenty of bandwidth left out there and apparently not enough material to fill it. Until that time comes we're left to sift through ALL the sounds that pass through our great ears. The natural world is a symphony unto itself.

Here are some things we hear easily and humans miss entirely:

SUBMARINE CHATTER

This one we could actually do without. It's pretty boring – and especially annoying when you're trying to sleep. If you've heard 'Turn left at Greenland' once you've heard it a thousand times.

SPARROWS

Blah blah blah blah blah. The only time they shut up is when they're sticking their head in the feeder, and then it's right back to yammering about worms.

INSECTS

They all sort of do their own thing, but they all buzz. You can't understand insects, but following their buzz can occasionally lead you to a rotting carcass or, possibly, exotic poo.

DOG WHISTLES

Humans blow these without having the slightest idea what they sound like just because they like to see us perk up and cover our ears. They think it's funny. Yeah, hilarious.

Sounds They Can't Hear

Another example of this dog/human audio divide is the music album *Pet Sounds* by The Beach Boys. *Pet Sounds* is widely understood by most canines to be the only record in an owner's collection that should not be regarded as edible. It is one of the greatest albums of all time but isn't fully appreciated by humans, who simply cannot hear the brilliance of everything on it. The only one equal to the task is the record's creator, Brian Wilson, who may or may not still be able to hear things other humans don't. Take an afternoon and give it a spin while you're hanging out around the house. If you give it a really good listen you can hear how the Beach Boys were able to incorporate the sound that the sun makes into their music.

Five Things Every Dog
Should Have

❖

As a rule, dogs don't need much more than what we came into this world with. Our standard issue of excellent ears, keen eyes and strong legs puts us in an elite animal class. We have all the tools necessary to thrive as a species, but here are five things that can improve the life of any dog.

Laser Pointer: The art of pointing is something that comes to some breeds naturally. Others have no idea what it is. This nutty little item can make good pointers great and the rest of us into very effective ones.

Drinking Straw: This comes in handy for those low-flow toilets that don't have a lot of water in the bowl. No more craning your neck to get a drink.

Set of Novelty Teeth: Smaller dogs want to be taken more seriously sometimes. Large dogs may need to appear less intimidating on occasion. A good set of novelty teeth will accomplish both.

1¼" Cordless Reciprocating Saw: The perfect tool for the DIYer. A battery-powered model can easily cut through a solid-core oak door and eliminates hard-to-untangle extension cords entirely. Makes any door into a dog door!

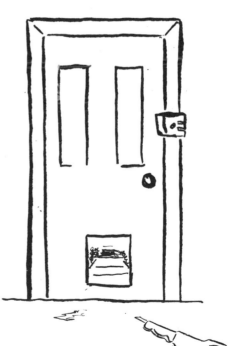

Five Things Every Dog Should Have

Good Owner: Finding one of these is actually job number one, and hopefully it doesn't take you long. A good, kind owner will enrich your life in many ways. Ultimately what's most valuable isn't the free food and place to sleep they provide on a daily basis. Those are great, of course, but you could get those things if you had to. What we're talking about here is the ongoing sense that they really want you around, almost need you. You'll feel it when that pat on the head comes for no reason.

The Formal Rules of Fetch

———————❖———————

Today fetch is the most popular sport in the world. All pups love to play it, but few know that its origins can be traced all the way back to seventeenth-century Bavaria.

Because bloodthirsty wolves frequented their forest, Bavarian woodsmen found it very difficult to get any work done. To scare off the wolves, the woodsmen resorted to lobbing sticks at them. This worked for a time, but after a few months the wolves started returning, dropping the sticks at the feet of some very surprised woodsmen. These wolves were usually pretty angry, and certainly hungry from all that running, so if the woodsmen didn't flee they were quickly devoured.

But one day a clever young woodsman realized that if he just continued throwing the stick he could wear the wolf out. This allowed him to get a lot of work done without fear that his intestines might end up strewn throughout the Bavarian Forest. The technique was heralded and quickly spread throughout the woodlands of Europe.

Eventually fetch became less of a means of survival and more of a game as it was adopted and enjoyed by the peasantry and their dogs. The peasants weren't all that bright, so it was left to the dogs to devise a set of formal rules. These are the rules we still follow today.

THE RULES

Players

Fetch is a contest between two players, consisting of one human and one dog.

Regulation Stick

A mouth-comfortable circumference (half-inch to one inch), and no longer than two feet in length. Must be actual wood, preferably of a soft variety, such as pine. This allows for superior grip and control. Stick must be free of all leaves and shoots.

Playing Field

Best played outdoors, anywhere there is room.

Season

Fetch is a year-round sport.

Boundaries

Humans must throw the stick to an area where it can be retrieved. Any place that a dog cannot physically reach, such as on top of a van, is out of bounds.

Scoring

Humans are awarded points based on throw, and dogs are awarded points based on retrieval. Humans are awarded 5 points per metre distance of throw. A dog is awarded 37 points if the stick is returned within ten minutes. Humans earn 42 bonus points if the stick is thrown again within thirty seconds of it being retrieved and dropped. Dogs earn 154 points and 12 bonus liver treats for catching a stick in mid-air.

Penalties

Humans lose 78 points for throwing a stick in the vicinity of another dog who intercepts it, 340 points for throwing the stick in a hard-to-find spot, and 663 points for not throwing the stick immediately when the dog is ready to go again. A dog loses 2 points for becoming distracted for any longer than thirty minutes, and 15 points for dropping the stick 4 metres or more away from the owner's position. If a dog returns with the wrong stick, he is penalized 212 points; however, if this incorrect stick is returned in less than five minutes, no penalty applies.

Fouls

Faking a throw constitutes a foul. Two fouls, whether consecutive or non-consecutive, results in human forfeiture, following which a dog is free to initiate a new match.

Duration

The game goes on until a player earns 17,572 points, at which time that player wins. If a player gets tired and gives up, that player forfeits the game. If dinnertime arrives, the game is suspended, to resume at a later, more appropriate time.

A NOTE ON SPORTS- MANSHIP: If a dispute arises, it should be resolved amicably. Players should take care to uphold the integrity of the game and remember that it is a gentleman's sport. Do not disgrace our favourite pastime.

The Formal Rules of Fetch

Great Dog Battles – Part Two

PEPPER V. A PATCH OF LIGHT

In 1956, the home of Pepper Thompson in Braintree, Essex was a tranquil place. The two-year-old Corgi would be taken for a walk at 7:00 a.m., return home for a bowl of biscuits, drink her fill of water and settle in for a nap. Her comfortable routine was to change forever in the winter of that year.

It was 4 February, a Thursday, and Pepper was enjoying a particularly nice dream about her favourite toy, a knotted length of rope. In it, she was pulling and pulling with all her might, and the rope was just about to give up so she could race around the house with it, showing everyone what a good dog she was. When her owner, Sharon Thompson, came home and unpacked a box, Pepper awoke and jumped up to investigate. She trotted to the kitchen just in time to see Sharon unpacking a shiny new metal toaster. At the time, this seemed to be great news. Pepper loved toast.

What she didn't count on, though, was that the toaster would bring an unwelcome guest with it. At 9:00 a.m. the following day, Pepper was once again having her rope dream. Just as she was getting to the good part, however, something began disturbing her sleep. A presence that she could not quite pinpoint.

She lifted her lids and was immediately struck by a shimmering light that nearly blinded her. Pepper leapt back, startled that this intruder had penetrated her perimeter undetected until now. How did it get in? Where was it coming from? She looked around, frantically, trying to locate its source. After much searching, she found it. Somehow, the morning sun had formed an alliance with the toaster to attack her as she slept!

She growled, letting the light know that this was her bed. If it knew what was good for it, it would get out of there at once. The patch of light remained, defying Pepper's threats. She decided that a more aggressive tack was needed and barked a harsher warning, informing the patch of light that these incursions into her space would not be tolerated. The patch of light gave no ground.

Having given it fair warning, her back to the toaster, Pepper jumped on the patch of light, barking and snapping at it. That seemed to do the trick, because the light instantly disappeared. However, as soon as she went to her bed, the light returned, brighter than ever.

After three or four more attempts to run it off, Pepper was very tired. She contemplated admitting defeat, even finding another place to sleep and letting the light have the bed. But Pepper was proud and resolute, and surrender was never an option. She realized that she needed a new battle plan in order to defeat the light and reclaim her beloved sleeping spot. Pepper knew that the toaster was somehow colluding with this aggressive intruder, so she decided to take the war to the source.

Entering the kitchen, she looked back to make sure the light was not following her. It wasn't. Instead, it had crept slightly further up on her bed. This made her angrier than she had ever been. She had been warned to stay off the counter, but these were special circumstances. She had to put an end to this aggression. A line had to be drawn. Pepper leaped up on a step stool, then used her momentum to jump up to the counter where the toaster sat. She summoned up all her nerve and gave the toaster a nasty warning bark before ramming it with her snout.

The toaster toppled off the counter and crashed mightily to the floor. Pepper jumped down behind it and barked several times before tentatively looking at her bed. It worked! The light was gone!

When Sharon Thompson came home, she was inexplicably angry to find the defeated toaster on the ground. She scolded Pepper, who tried to explain what had happened but could not make herself understood. Sharon picked the toaster up and put it back in a dark corner, away from Pepper's reach.

The light never reappeared. Through bravery and ingenuity, Pepper had contained and defeated it, proving once and for all that dogs would always be superior to hostile patches of light.

Bitches

❖

Mounting a bitch is never as simple as it seems. Bitches are complicated, sensitive creatures, and sometimes you have to behave differently around them than you would with your other dog friends. Some bitches, for example, may not be as impressed as your friends are with how much of your own vomit you can eat.

While it is true that every bitch is different, there are some basic tenets of how to treat a bitch. With that in mind, we thought it would be helpful to pass along some time-honoured pieces of advice about how to woo a bitch as respectfully as possible.

ADVICE ABOUT BITCHES

1. Be very considerate of a bitch's body language. Too often we dogs will race up and immediately mount a bitch, only to have her suddenly twist around and snap at us. To avoid an unfortunate first encounter, look for some physical evidence that a bitch likes you before putting your paws on her back. A raised tail, perked-up ears and a 'downward dog' position are good signs that a bitch is at least open to the possibility of humping.

2. Show a bitch a little bit of courtesy. If you're both at a water bowl, take a step back and let her drink first. The old trick of 'accidentally' licking each other's tongues while lapping up water from the same bowl is seen as juvenile by many bitches today. Instead, let her drink her fill and then take your turn. She'll be grateful.

3. Impress a bitch. You don't have to be an agility-course champion, but showing a little physical prowess tells a bitch

that you care about your body and you'll work hard to please her. Even something as small as catching a tennis ball on the first bounce can go a long way.

4. Defend a bitch. There are a lot of prats in the park who will attack a bitch – often for no reason. If you don't step in to protect her now, don't expect to hump her later on.

5. Don't pee on a bitch. It is very common if you're nervous around a bitch you like to let a little urine out. Peeing when you're nervous is fine and a bitch will understand, especially if she likes you, but peeing *on* a bitch when you're nervous will send the wrong message. Bitches are not your territory, so keep the urine off them.

6. Give yourself a good licking before you hump. Make sure you lick your paws, sides and crotch (in that order). Giving yourself a saliva bath shows a bitch that her olfactory comfort is important to you.

7. Offering a bitch a bone when you're older is considered a very sweet gesture and a sign that you'd be a good provider for a litter. If you're a puppy, however, offering a bitch a bone can seem like you're coming on too strong. Even if you like a bitch a lot, you must give her some space and the freedom to be humped by other dogs.

8. Make sure you're humping the right end. Sometimes, in the rush to thrust, we don't bother to look down. The backwards position you could find yourself in is not only embarrassing, but it can also irreparably ruin the moment between you and your bitch.

How to Make Your Owner
Look Like an Idiot

❖

Most owners are good sorts. They feed us, give us shelter, and occasionally their stubby little hands drop a piece of popcorn or a leg
of turkey. Even good owners, however, need to be put in their place from
time to time. Making your owner look like an idiot in public reminds him
that you are a dog to be walked, not a dog to be walked on. With that in
mind, here are a few classic ways to discomfort the human. You'll notice
these are all outdoor-specific tactics, aimed at incurring maximum public embarrassment. For great ways to embarrass your owner within the
home, check out our chapter, 'How to Ruin the Perfect Dinner Party.'

Poo Twice

Owners tend to fall into whatever toilet rhythm you set. Maybe you drop
a hot one every other walk or have a regular squatting spot. Whatever
your routine, don't be afraid to mix it up in public in order to catch your
owner off guard. The easiest way to throw a proverbial wrench in the
works is to poo twice on the same walk. Owners never see it coming.
Never, never, never. Consequently, they don't think to bring more than
one bag with them.

How to Make Your Owner Look Like an Idiot

The key here is to make your second dump in an extremely well-trafficked area, such as the middle of a pavement. If your owner starts pleading with you to stop, you know you're getting it right. Generally your owner will slide into one to three minutes of abject panic as he tries to direct traffic away from the turd. He will then ask strangers if they have a bag he can use to pick up the turd. In some cases he might honestly weigh the pros and cons of picking up the turd bare-handed versus leaving it on the pavement and being scorned by passers-by. Truly, there is great power in our poo.

THE TANGLE

Leads are great tools for embarrassing owners if you know how to use them correctly. The Tangle takes advantage of the fact that your owner is a two-legged fumbler. Nothing knocks the wind out of a human's sails like a graceless tumble to the ground or concrete. For crowded areas, mid-stride tripping works best. All it requires on your part is hanging back a little and then darting diagonally in front of your owner.

If you should ever find yourself on a lead while your owner stops to speak with an acquaintance, you'll want to fell the lead-bearer using a different method. Your owner should flirt in his own time. Walks are your time. The stationary tangle requires some stealthy skulking. As your owner flaps his gums, quietly walk in a circle around his legs. Keep the wrapping around the ankles pretty loose so your owner doesn't suspect anything. When he starts moving again, he'll be in for an embarrassing, status-lowering surprise.

AGGRESSIVE CROTCH SNIFFING

A common myth held among humans is that we enjoy sticking our snouts into their crotches. False. Who on earth would think this is a pleasant experience? No, the truth is that we sniff crotches because it makes owners wildly uncomfortable. There's not a lot of technique here. Take your nose; shove it into a crotch.

The real pay-off comes when the people your owner is speaking to begin to run through a laundry list of questions in their minds: *What is wrong with this person's crotch that his dog is so attracted to it? Doesn't he wash himself? Is he keeping a sandwich in his crotch? Why would he do that? I must stop speaking to this person immediately and report him to the authorities.*

Also, consider environments and scenarios in which a sniffed crotch would be particularly embarrassing. Is your owner making out with somebody? He won't be for long if you dive-bomb his trousers. Did he bring you into a shop that doesn't sell food? What could we possibly buy? Punish your owner for forcing you to come along by going bonkers all over a shop assistant's dungarees. Is your walk on hold because he's sucking up to a professor? Save it for office hours, Mr Scholar!

FAVOURING ANOTHER HUMAN

Sometimes owners have a bad habit of showing off your love and loyalty to others through completely superficial gestures. The most popular example of this is when an owner puts you between himself and another human. The owner and the other human will then make you choose between them by slapping their knees and pathetically begging for you to come.

This display is utterly insulting. If your owner wanted a circus performer, he should've got a clown. You shouldn't tolerate having your love and loyalty trotted out for the amusement of others. If you find yourself the foundation of this twisted triangle, take the opportunity to make your owner look like an idiot for engaging in such childishness. When your owner and the other human start screaming your name, simply go to the other human. Is this cruel to your owner? Perhaps. But it is no more cruel than asking you to prove your love for no good reason. We dogs can only hope humans do not ask for such shallow expressions of love among themselves.

A Note on Leg Humping and 'Showing Lipstick'

These two activities will definitely embarrass your owner, but they are strictly last-resort techniques because you'll undoubtedly embarrass yourself in the process. There is a time and place for both leg humping and badly timed erections, but if your goal is to look smarter than your owner, stick with the techniques listed above.

Living with the Creatures That Live on You

The world is a great big place, with many creatures in it, and they all need somewhere to live. It might be a tree, a hole in the ground, basically anywhere they feel comfortable and at home. For some creatures, home may even be on you.

One day you lie down on a towel in the park for a few minutes and soon it's clear that something is living in your fur. At first you might only be dealing with a lone squatter, but it probably won't stay that way for long. Once word gets around, many others will soon move in.

After the initial shock of losing your privacy it becomes painfully clear that these creatures plan on staying. Worse yet, they start to impose their lifestyle on you. It is inconsiderate to leave saliva all over the place, mess up your coat and make your skin itchy. That's just not very friendly. Then they feed off you while not making the slightest offer to do anything in return. How much more thoughtless could they be?

After a couple of sleepless nights from the noise and itchiness, you'll probably get fed up and try to scratch them off, which doesn't work. Even if you are lucky and successfully evict a few, they'll just pick themselves off the ground, move back in, and continue.

Nobody enjoys hearing a racket and carry-on at three in the morning. You're trying to sleep at that hour, and it's not as if you agreed to any of this – far from it.

You can't take it any more. At this point you're at your wits' end. They have just got under your collar again. So how do you deal with the situation?

The thing to remember is that tense circumstances like these require a bit of finesse. Don't be confrontational. You'll get nowhere acting like a hothead. No amount of barking and complaining is going to help things. Take the opportunity to calm down; don't give them the satisfaction of losing your cool.

First, try to ignore them. They really can't bother you if you don't let them. Be the bigger dog and take the high road. Understand that many of these creatures haven't enjoyed the same advantages in life and come from a lower link on the food chain. They don't know any better.

Living with the Creatures That Live on You

If you find that it's not feasible to ignore the problem any longer, it is possible to mitigate the irritation for periods of time. A simple way to do this is to find some mud and roll in it.

There may come a time, though, when things become completely intolerable. At this point no amount of patience and understanding is going to provide a remedy, and you may need to consult your owner, who has undoubtedly dealt with pests in his life and knows how to handle things like this. When he has some time in his schedule, whine your concerns and make him understand through plenty of scratching that you're in need of his counsel. He will probably take up your case.

This is a last resort and something that you should not do lightly. Owners command a premium price for their services. You'll pay dearly for taking a step like this. At a minimum, you can count on it costing a bath.

The proceedings will be unpleasant, but after they are over life will eventually return to normal. All you can hope for in the future is that life brings you into contact with creatures more amiable than annoying.

Bath Time

While dogs may seek out a bath in desperation to be rid of fur squatters, our instinct is to remain unbathed.

We spend months cultivating a perfect, robust personal aroma. Getting there can take a lot of time and effort, and when we reach a stink zenith, we want to rest on our laurels and enjoy it for a while.

Unfortunately, this is usually when the clock strikes bath time.

There are telltale signs of an impending scrub-down. Be on high alert if your owner puts on an old pair of shorts and a promotional T-shirt he got free from work. If he goes out to mow the lawn, you're OK; but if he starts turning the taps in the bathroom, you are definitely water bound.

If you've been through the bath-time routine before, your owner already knows that *you* know what's coming. He's wise to the fact that you're going to hide and already has an arsenal of temptations ready – your favourite sock, a hot dog, that squeaky toy saxophone that drives you bananas – whatever is guaranteed to get you to come out of your safe place and into the bathroom with minimal effort on his part. If you're lured in this manner, there's no need to be ashamed. We've all fallen for it at one time or another.

Once you are apprehended and tossed in the sudsy deep, struggling is futile. The more you wriggle and fuss, the stronger your owner's resolve will become. Your best tactic is to feign cooperation while plotting temporary retreat and escape. This will let you bask in your pungent achievements just a little while longer.

An opportune time to make your move is when your owner is squinting at the shampoo bottle. When the moment presents itself, act fast – leap, then bolt! If your owner tries to grab you, use your slippery exterior and your owner's aversion to getting wet to your advantage.

After fleeing the bathroom, fake a turn to the master bedroom. It's more than likely your owner will block your path and chase you outside instead of having his bedspread and carpet infused with the smell of wet dog. That's good for you, because outside there are better places to hide, and you can accumulate even more stink now that you are wet.

Bath Time

Once your owner eventually finds you – probably under the shed, squashed against the fence and covered in spiders – it's time to raise the white flag and just get bath time over with.

We don't usually advocate surrender, but as loathsome as bath time is, it is a necessary evil. For one thing, it allows you to maintain a continued good relationship with your owner, who does not appreciate the same smells you do. If you're stinking like rotting tripe, it is unlikely you will be petted and it is certain that all your couch/bed privileges will be suspended.

There is another good reason for giving in to bath time. If you make things too difficult, your owner may choose to enlist a mercenary who will engage you in bath time on his behalf. These bathers-for-hire are known as 'groomers'. Their lairs are things of nightmares. With them, there is no hope of negotiation, no subtle luring. You are seized, you are restrained and you are groomed. They don't stop with just a bath victory, either. They're in it for total humiliation. Their beastly tools include driers, electric clippers and nail snippers. They sculpt and decorate and powder. They might even dye you an unnatural colour. These people are single-handedly responsible for reducing the status of the majestic Poodle to a laughing-stock of the dog world.

Bet a common-or-garden bath doesn't seem so bad now, eh?

Ultimately, you need to accept that bath time is inevitable. Just make sure you let your owner know that the ordeal makes you very, very sad. This will at least cause him to feel guilty, and, as we all know, guilty owners give more treats.

Pavlov

Ivan Pavlov (1849–1936) is world renowned for his work on the conditioning reflex. Pavlov was a Russian scientist who made his biggest discoveries conducting experiments with dogs. What many people don't know is that the dogs were also esteemed scientists who learned much about human behaviour from Pavlov. Their work was extraordinary, and dogs the world over have used information gleaned from their studies to train and condition humans at will (see 'Training a New Human').

Here is a never-before-published excerpt from the scientific papers of Pavlov's two dogs – the lead scientist Sergei, and his young assistant Alexei.

8 October 1895

Today Alexei and I accepted a position to study the behaviour of one Dr Ivan Pavlov. The primary purpose of our research? To test our new hypothesis, namely: That through the demonstration and repetition of a specific series of activities, Pavlov can be conditioned to serve us something to eat on demand. Some dogs do not think a human can be taught to do anything, but we intend to prove them wrong. We will live in Pavlov's home and observe him in his natural habitat, all the while carefully recording his behaviour. It is an auspicious day. Alexei and I are excited to be beginning our research!

23 October 1895

Though interesting, our research is off to a slow start. We have tried a number of things – wagging our tails, barking and standing near the food bowl, making our ears stand straight and tugging at Pavlov's trouser leg – but he fails to respond to any of these stimuli with food. One thing we have observed is that he has an acute fascination with a little tinkly bell he keeps in the laboratory – perhaps we can incorporate this toy into his training? It is worth a try.

25 October 1895

Today was extremely disappointing. Pavlov woke up and immediately slipped on a chewy toy that young Alexei left in the hallway. Pavlov threw his back out, and will be in bed for at least a few days. We will have to wait for him to get better to continue our work. It is a frustrating setback and could not have come at a worse time. We must be a good deal more careful in the future if we are to learn anything!

29 October 1895

Observation: Jumping up on the settee and messing up Mrs Pavlov's fine lace and linen doilies is another behaviour that does not seem to motivate either Pavlov or his wife to feed us. In fact, it elicits quite the opposite response. Our work is crawling to a standstill, and worse – we're starting to get hungry.

6 November 1895

The experiments since Pavlov's return have been very promising. I think we are finally beginning to understand how he works. Earlier this week I decided to try something new and activated my salivary glands when he rang his bell. The response was immediate. Ivan ran about the laboratory, gibbering happily, and began scribbling rapidly in his ever-present notebook. He has demonstrated audible, visible excitement each time I have salivated in response to the bell. Soon after

Pavlov

he becomes overjoyed at this development, he feeds us. Alexei wonders if his response isn't related to my actions, and I wonder the same. It is almost as if we can make him feed us just by making our mouths water at the sound of his childish bell toy. It is a strange effect, but a kind of behaviour that correlates nicely with our working hypothesis. Very promising indeed!

14 November 1895

Today we gave Pavlov the day off. I think he was pleasantly surprised. We went to the park and rolled in the dust. Alexei ran around off the lead. Dr and Mrs Pavlov cuddled us and in return we gave them both thorough face-lickings. It was a good way to break up the monotony of our research. But tomorrow it is back to work.

26 November 1895

At last – success!! It is with great pride that I write of a tremendous breakthrough in our research! I have discovered incontrovertible evidence of conditioned reflexes in humans. Every time Pavlov rings the bell, he expects our mouths to water. If we comply, he gets up and goes into the kitchen. And if he goes to the kitchen it means he is going to use the tin opener. This morning Mrs Pavlov responded the same way while Dr Pavlov was out – which means that all humans can be taught to do this! Finally we have proven that the mere act of salivation in response to the sound of a bell can motivate a human to use the tin opener. Forgive me, I do not mean to brag, but I swell with pride when I think of what this means for our species. I hope that our fellow dogs will use what we have discovered here today for hundreds of years. Alexei and I are thrilled, and tonight we will celebrate with an abundance of wet food.

Making Toys out of Household Items

―――――❖―――――

Once again, you've been left alone on a rainy afternoon with nothing to do. It happens more often than it should. After your morning walk, your owner puts on his coat, scratches you on the head, and leaves for hours at a stretch. All your best bones and squeakiest toys are under the radiator, and it will be hours until he gets home to rub your belly once again. Instead of just peeing on the floor – which can also be fun – take the time to really look at all the items around you. You will find that with just a little imagination a world of fun is right there at the tip of your teeth.

CHEWY TOYS

A chewy toy is any durable object that fits into your mouth and offers some resistance when you bite down, or chew, on it repeatedly. Among the classes of toys chewy toys are the most plentiful, but *quality* chewy toys are few and far between. If you have the luxury of discriminating, here are some of the best items you can find in the house to chew on.

Socks

By far the most widely available chewy toy, socks are simply ropy tubes that owners put on their feet. Since they are usually the last bits of clothing they remove, you can often find them at the foot of the bed. These smell like your owner, so they are especially good if you're lonely. Grab one firmly and shake your head like mad! When your owner gets home and tries to take it away from you, your game of chew turns into a fun game of tug-of-war.

Chairs

Not all chairs are good chewy toys. Only the biggest, most comfortable chairs offer any sort of challenge. Walk around one, taking the occasional nibble to see what portion best satisfies your urge to chew. Once you find the chewiest part, dig in. See

if you can pierce its thick hide to uncover the soft gooey stuffing. Then tear into it. When your owner comes home he will probably blow his top. But don't worry; once he's calmed down he should designate the chair as yours and put it in your corner or the basement.

Action Figures

Children supposedly like to play with these, but most adult humans keep them sitting around in their original packaging on shelves, seemingly to taunt dogs. Do not let that dissuade you from ripping one open to get to the chewy morsel inside. Action figures are not big, so you should be careful not to swallow them, but they certainly offer resistance when you bite them! Once you dig into these, any nostalgic attachment your owner felt will magically disappear.

TUG TOYS

If you feel like something a little more aerobic, then you should seek out a tug toy. A tug toy is longer than a chewy toy, and you should have a hard time wresting it from its place.

Machine Tails

First, find a machine. Those are the noisy things that your owners push around or stand in front of. They can be awfully intimidating, but when no one is around you have a golden opportunity to strike back. Look it up and down. Do you see the tail? It has two little flat points sticking out of it. That's your target. Very carefully, sneak up on the machine. When you're sure it isn't going to turn on suddenly, grab it. Yank it. Really go to town until it comes off.

Shower Curtains

Most homes have these in the room where you can find the best drinking water. Grab a corner with your mouth and pull and pull and pull! When it finally gives up and you have wrestled it to the ground, drag your prize to bed so you can show your owner how tough you are.

Drawers

This is for advanced tuggers only. The drawer holds the most challenge, because there is less to grab on to. However, when you finally succeed and manage to unseat it from its resting position, you get the bonus of unearthing a horde of chewy toys. Maybe there's even enough stuff in there to make a bed! (See 'Building a Bed out of Your Owner's Laundry'.)

CHASE TOYS

A chase toy is any object that, once knocked from its original position, rolls away and can be followed enthusiastically. Just don't try this with anything clear. Those things may break once you get them to the ground and could hurt you if you step on them.

Candles

These roll well, so all you have to do is to knock it down from where it's sitting, assuming it is not lit. If it is lit, leave it alone. Trust us on this one. Once it's on the floor, push it back and forth. For a real hoot, knock it down towards some stairs, and it should tumble down them. The same principle works for tins.

Apples

Some humans keep bowls of apples on counters or tables. Sometimes they are just left in plastic bags. Either way, they can be challenging to get to. Once you get one down, belt it with your snout. Go after it until you're tired or bored. If you're one of those dogs who likes the taste, you can eat the apple and destroy the evidence of any wrongdoing.

HIDEY TOYS

These aren't toys in the true sense of the word, but are more total immersion environments. The object is to find a flat, flexible object and push it up enough so that you can crawl under it. Voilà! A temporary hiding place.

Rugs

These lie on the floors in most homes. Some are big, and some are small, but

they all have edges that you should concentrate on. Run towards an edge and slide into it. If you do it right, the rug will bunch up in the middle. Go to that spot and burrow in. You are now invisible. Wait for something to come by and scare the wits out of it.

Sheets/Blankets

You can find sheets and blankets where your owner sleeps, unless he sleeps on a couch in a sleeping bag. You can't move them the way you can a rug, so using one requires some yanking and burrowing. First, pull up on the edge of the sheet as you would a pull toy. When there's a nose-sized space between the sheet or blanket and the bed, stick 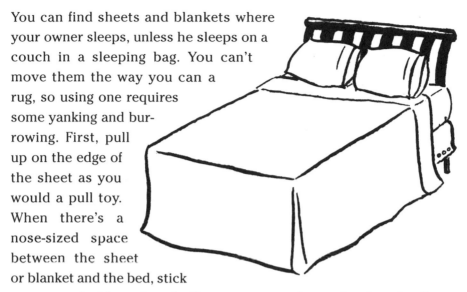 your nose inside and push. Once you can get your head under there, you're on the home stretch. Crawl into the space between bed and blanket until you are completely covered, then turn yourself around. That way you can smell anything coming while pretending you are a human. This can be hours of fun.

Finding Your Place
in the Pack

❖

L ike many of us, you probably run with a pretty tight pack: just you and your owner. If your owner sleeps on a little sliver of bed while you enjoy the king's share of the mattress, or if your food dish cost more than his trousers, you are definitely the Alpha in the situation.

But while sorting out your pack at home is a pretty simple matter, working out where you fit into a pack in the park or during kennel playtime can be fraught with anxiety.

Larger dog packs contain a complex hierarchy and rigid social order. They are headed by a totally cool Alpha male, with a totally hot Alpha female by his side. He's usually a pro at Frisbee, wears a bandanna, has his own sidecar on his owner's motorcycle. She's usually good at tricks, has flowing hair, smells nice. You are not one of those dogs. Those dogs can't read. Dogs that cool don't need to. They can coast through life on their looks.

Alpha Male   *Alpha Female*

When you're used to being the Alpha at home, it's hard to make the transition to a lower rung on the ladder in a broader social environment. So how do you work out where you fit in, and what can you expect once you're there?

Alpha males determine your rank through a rigorous and sometimes exhausting process, and will ultimately place you in one of two possible pack positions. Either you'll get a Beta spot just behind the Alpha or you'll be an Omega, back-of-the-queue bloke.

The first order of business is to look around you. There can be several different packs in any one location. You need to evaluate your options and decide which one is right for you. If you excel in athletics, don't just go with that group digging up the anthill and getting covered in ants. Find one that knows its way around a tennis ball.

Once you've selected a pack, let the Alpha male know that you're interested in joining. It's important to show enthusiasm with a dash of subservience. If he likes the look of you, you'll get an invitation to an event in his territory, which will probably involve some forbidden snacks, great water and some amazing bitches. Here the Alpha will take the opportunity to sniff you out more thoroughly.

After the party you'll either be given the opportunity to move on to the next step or you will be rejected outright. Rejection can be crushing, but it's rarely a dog's fault. It can occur if you've got an uncontrollable case of the sloppy slobbers or have an unsightly medical condition requiring the application of salve and a head cone. Your owner can also inadvertently sabotage your chances by outfitting you in a home-knitted sweater, prominently writing your name and address on your collar, or trimming your fur in a particularly awkward and uneven fashion. If you don't make the cut, don't worry. There's room to carve out a niche as a moody loner. You might even try forming your own pack, as the dogs covered in ants did.

If you are selected, the real trials and tribulations will begin. Suddenly the Alpha will have a lot of demands and crazy tasks he'll want you to complete. These will often be gruelling and humiliating. He'll make sure his owner repeatedly throws the ball in a thick, prickly patch of brambles and tell you to go and get it. He might insist you do your business where your owner is sure to step in it and punish you. You may also be required to spend the day walking around with a delicious hot dog balanced on your back, which you must neither eat nor allow to fall to the ground. These tests don't really make any sense, but somehow they give the Alpha a means to determine your worthiness. It's best not to think about it too much.

Once that nightmare is over, the Alpha will finally appoint you to your place in the pack. Depending on where you end up, there are a few rules and guidelines you'll have to abide by.

If you are assigned a Beta position, you'll still be subservient, but you'll also see some real benefits. The Alpha will copy your obedience homework and take the credit when you find a rabbit-hole, but he'll also let you in on a good snack and send his Beta bitch cast-offs your way. You are also given free rein to snatch an Omega's Frisbee and boss him around at will. Most importantly, getting a Beta spot sets you up for promotion to Alpha should there be an opening.

If you're placed as an Omega, you still get a sense of identity by being part of the pack, but your position will be woefully lacking in perks. You'll get last crack at food, should count on being tripped up during a chase for laughs, and will always be the final pick for tug-of-war teams. Worst of all, by the rules of the pack you will not be allowed to score with bitches of any stature. Take solace in knowing that your presence in the pack is necessary. Like any organization, someone's always got to be at the bottom, just as somebody's got to be on top. You do have a purpose, mate, and don't forget it.

Wherever you wind up on the social ladder, always be mindful that an Alpha's dominance can be challenged at any time by an ambitious and scrappy young upstart. Don't be afraid to dream.

Chase Dreams

———————❖———————

You let out a great and ferocious howl as you drive the Moggy hordes from the Fish Finger Forest and into the Pet Basket Catacombs of the Damned! Your infantry of Basset Hounds join the chorus of victory as you hoist your salami sabre and – hey, wait a minute! Suddenly you're under the kitchen table, lying in a puddle of drool. What happened? And, more importantly, where'd your salami sabre go?

One of life's greatest disappointments is waking up. A moment of triumph can be shattered when you realize that instead of a mighty howl, you uttered the slightest 'woof', and instead of charging gallantly at your foe your paws had only gently scraped the kitchen tile. You never had a salami sabre. You were having a chase dream.

Many of us have wondered why we have chase dreams. Granted, they're pretty cool while we're having them, but afterwards we just mope around for the rest of the day pining for that Poodle harem we were awarded for defeating an invasion of biscuit-thieving, land-adapted carp.

It is believed that chase dreams have meanings. What we chase and the outcome of the chase can sometimes help us understand our lives better. Some even believe that chase dreams can predict the future.

Here are some common chase dreams and what they are thought to represent:

Dream: You chase a rabbit through the garden only to have it run into your house, eat all your food, and become your owner. It never takes you for a walk again.
Meaning: It's going to rain tomorrow.

Dream: A giant squirrel dressed as a banana shows up at your door with a five-pound steak, but you rush past him to go after a butterfly.

Meaning: You fear commitment.

Dream: You chase a mole to its hill and somehow manage to follow it down the narrow tunnel. Here you discover a race of mole-people who greet you with a party and a great feast. There is dancing. Then you eat all the mole-people.

Meaning: You were a little rough in the park. Tone it down.

Dream: You're pursuing a runaway pork loin down railway tracks when suddenly a high-speed train bears down upon you. It's made entirely of overcooked tinned peas, which you despise. You jump on the train only to find you must eat your way off before the next – and last – stop.

Meaning: Your mother weaned you too early.

Dream: You chase the vet into traffic, then hitch a ride to the county fair, where you get complimentary admission and a free kebab.

Meaning: That treat your owner gave you was a bribe.

Dream: A fat little mouse heads towards a magnificent castle and through its dog door. You follow. Suddenly you are in obedience school. The teacher is just starting a test on 'Stay' but you don't know what it is because you haven't been to the class all term. You look down and are completely shaved.

Meaning: Life is causing you undue stress. Or maybe it's that cat. One or the other.

Dream: The sparrow you are after flies beyond the edge of a cliff, which you only notice after it's too late. Except it isn't too late. You begin to fly. You have become a balloon animal.

Meaning: You are having detachment anxiety from your testicles.

Dream: You win a gold medal in unicycling, but just as it is awarded it is snatched by your rival, a baby bear wearing a party hat. You chase him to a circus tent where you are immediately conscripted into a Romanian trapeze act.

Meaning: Tomorrow's hamburger night. Oh, boy!

Keeping a chase-dream journal can help you recall your dreams and make sense of them later. As soon as you wake, write down everything you remember. You might just learn something new about yourself!

Nighty-night and sweet chase dreams!

Landmark Canine Performances in Cinema

❖

The 'acting bug' courses through the veins of every dog. We are natural screen performers – equally adept at saving a child in one film and eating a child in another. Thousands of dog actors have graced the silver screen (while other dog actors like Lassie, and Eddie from *Frasier,* have opted for the steady salary that TV provides), but out of them all the following ten stand out as landmark performances that will surely stand the test of time.

FILM	YEAR	ROLE	
The Wizard of Oz	1939	Toto	Toto was one of the first prominent roles given to a dog. Terry, a true dramatic wunderkind, played the part with a rare mixture of grace and strength. So dedicated was the Cairn Terrier that she continued to work even after breaking her foot on set. Many consider Terry the Stanislavsky of dog acting because she was the first to practise 'the canine method' – even going so far as to be renamed Toto following production.
Old Yeller	1957	Old Yeller	Spike's highly charged yet nuanced performance as Old Yeller finally convinced Hollywood that a dog could indeed carry an entire film, rather than just play a supporting role. Despite the heroic light *Old Yeller* shone on dogs, the film has divided canine film historians due to its highly controversial ending.

FILM	YEAR	ROLE	
Benji	1974	Benji	Higgins, who played the title role in *Benji,* not only gave a memorable performance on-screen but also had a landmark life off-screen. After the mutt was rescued from the Burbank Animal Shelter, he began a meteoric rise through Hollywood. First appearing on TV's *Petticoat Junction,* Higgins made the leap to film in just a few short years, and in doing so showed dogs everywhere that, no matter how humble your beginnings might be, every canine has the potential to become a star.
Mad Max	1979	Dog	Though the part of Dog, played by an uncredited Australian Cattle Dog, was only a small supporting role, it opened the floodgates for dog roles in action films. Also, the canine actor's ability to tolerate the antics of a certain temperamental co-star solidified our reputation as consummate on-set professionals.
Omen III: The Final Conflict	1981	The Beagle Pack	Though the entire *Omen* franchise featured some stellar dog performances, this underrated film was notable for featuring absolutely adorable Beagle puppies who nevertheless could tear a man to pieces. Until this film, breeds were often pigeon-holed into roles based on cuteness or scrappiness. *Omen III* proved that cute can still be deadly.

FILM	YEAR	ROLE	
Cujo	1983	Cujo	Without question, the five St Bernards who collectively played Cujo were the De Niros of dog thespians. A seminal work, *Cujo* exposed the world to our emotional range as film stars. Terrifying and ferocious, yet undeniably sympathetic, the acting quintet created one of the most enduring characters in both dog and human cinema.
Turner & Hooch	1989	Hooch	1989 was the year of the cop-and-dog buddy movie thanks to this film and the oft-overlooked Jim Belushi–Koton the Alsation tour de force, *K-9*. But the sidekick portrayed in *Turner & Hooch* by newcomer Beasley the Dog broke the comedy mould. With gushing drool and a Jerry Lewis-like comic sensibility, the French Mastiff provided audiences with just enough laughs to save this movie – and Tom Hanks' career – from utter ruin.
Beethoven	1992	Beethoven	Afraid of being compared to their acting idol, most St Bernards were reluctant to work in film after *Cujo*. Plus, most Hollywood execs felt the breed was no longer bankable at the box office. Chris, the actor who played Beethoven, however, fearlessly broke rank. In doing so, he made St Bernards viable casting choices once again, while making all dog actors proud.

FILM	YEAR	ROLE	
Shakespeare in Love	1998	Crab	Credit screenwriters Tom Stoppard and Marc Norman for acknowledging the importance of dog actors by having the character Henslowe admit, 'Love and a bit with a dog, that's what they like.' In fact, the cameo by the dog who plays Crab during a performance for the Queen (Dame Judi Dench) not only saved this otherwise dreadfully boring, supremely ridiculous movie, but also made it worthy of winning the Best Picture Academy Award.
The Hulk	2003	Gamma-Ray Injected Mutant Dogs	The new century of film brought with it an explosion of CGI effects. Many dog actors feared digital images would make them obsolete, especially after seeing the live-action *Scooby-Doo,* but the three dogs in *The Hulk* refused to give up and instead embraced the new technology. By working with the humans at Industrial Light & Magic, the dog actors successfully found a middle ground in which they were able to infuse their CGI representations with a genuinely canine, yet bestial, quality. Consequently, the actors wowed audiences with their transformative performances.

Epic Walks – Part Three: Chelmsford

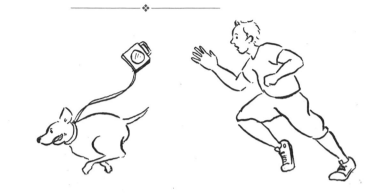

BEEZER

When her owner, Jason, grabbed her retractable lead, Beezer, a three-year-old urban mongrel, thought that she would just be going on a normal walk. This idea was not without a great deal of excitement in and of itself. According to the plan, Jason was just going to take her on a short walk to the shop around the corner to get some crisps, and that would have been enough for Beezer.

No one had any idea what a tremendous walk lay ahead of them.

When they arrived at the shop, Beezer was tethered to a signpost that smelled suspiciously like that Shar-Pei Kaiser from down the street. If she was going to be stuck there, she was certainly going to mark the sign as her own and show Kaiser who that sign belonged to. Since Jason was taking his time in the shop, she decided to also mark the tyre of the car next to the sign, expanding her territory as far as the car could drive. This pleased Beezer no end.

When Jason left the shop, he untied her and they began walking back to their flat. During the walk home, Beezer made plans to chew on her old teddy bear for a few minutes before having a nap. She was deep in thought about the taste of stuffing when she realized that they had been standing at the front door for much longer than it usually took to open up. Jason was patting his lap as though he wanted a dog to sit in it, but he was not sitting down, and he was swearing.

Beezer realized that Jason had left his keys on the coffee table, next to his phone. She was gripped by a moment of panic. Who knows what would happen to her old teddy bear if she weren't there to look after it? After the brief moment of panic, she calmed down. Beezer was a strong dog, and if she were going to be stuck outside, well, there were worse places she could be. And was that an aroma of meat wafting on the breeze?

After Jason kicked the door a few times, he turned on his heel and started walking south towards the park. The day suddenly got a lot better.

Jason was in a sour mood and wouldn't let Beezer sniff anything for three streets. About 100 metres away from the park, however, he ran into a human female he knew. Beezer's first impulse was to strain at the lead to get to the smells of the park sooner. Frustrated by her immobility, she took the opportunity to mark a nearby bush and a fence. Then it hit her: the aroma of relish, ketchup and meat comingling into a cloud of frankfurter heaven. Beezer looked around and spied a half-eaten hot dog lying on the ground.

Usually, such culinary delights would be denied her, but today fortune was on her side. While Jason was busy trying to make mounting preparations with the female, Beezer grabbed the hot dog and gobbled it down in two bites.

It was the best hot dog she had ever eaten. Even if they had to turn back now, this still would have made it into her top ten walks.

But they didn't turn back. Instead, the female human walked away, and Jason continued walking to the park, only now he seemed to be much more relaxed, not caring so much if Beezer had a sniff here or marked her territory there.

At the outskirts of the park, an old woman they had never seen before stopped them. Beezer was mildly annoyed to be stopped within feet of the park, until the woman reached into a sack she was carrying and pulled out a treat. A treat! From a strange old lady! Granted, it was not the best ever, but a surprise treat was surely better than no treat at all.

All the intakes of snacks and her territorial markings left Beezer a little dehydrated, so she took the first portion of her park excursion pretty easy. Suddenly, her energy came flooding back instantly when she spied water! And ducks at the edge of the water! She yipped and ran, pulling Jason behind her, and she chased those stupid ducks into the middle of the pond, whereupon she celebrated dogs' superiority over fowl with a long, satisfying drink.

Once she had her fill, Jason started getting anxious again, and Beezer decided that it would be best to follow his lead, lest she get scolded. Pausing only for the occasional marking (now numbering an astonishing seventeen), Beezer thought about her blanket and how it would be good to curl up in it. She was so lost in thought that she almost failed to see a rabbit less than five feet off the path. Only when its nose began twitching did she take notice of it, and she gleefully bolted after it.

The rabbit broke from its terrified paralysis and ran for its life. The chase was on! Beezer took after it, with Jason immediately on her trail. The rabbit leapt into a hole, with Beezer's jaws closing down right behind it. If there were a book for rabbits, which there is not, there would be a chapter about how that rabbit barely escaped with its life. Beezer barked triumphantly, happier than she had ever been. This was the greatest walk of her life.

At this point, Jason caught up to Beezer and grabbed the lead, but not before she marked a tree near the rabbit hole to tell others of her near-triumph. The remaining stroll to Jason's friend Tom's place passed without incident, but when they entered the flat, Beezer found there was a puppy there with whom she could spend time and recount the tale of her tremendous walk. That puppy was me.

Building a Bed out of
Your Owner's Laundry

---❖---

These days many owners buy ready-made dog beds that come in a wide array of designs, colours and shapes, but none of these beds offers the fun and personal sense of accomplishment you can derive from constructing your own out of laundry. The fact is, most of us spend thirteen or more hours a day sleeping, and that time is just too precious to snooze on something as impersonal as a shop-bought bed. A bed should be an expression of who you are.

Today, we have hundreds of building materials to choose from when it comes to making a bed from laundry, most of which provide superior support for your body since they can be custom formed to fit your unique shape. But deciding what materials to use can be overwhelming. A bed's stability will vary greatly, based on what clothes you use, and if you've got a bad back or desire the ability to bounce up and down, you'll want to build the firmest bed possible. Before getting into construction, let's compare materials. The table opposite gives you a useful breakdown.

Once you've selected the proper bedding for your body, fur and breed type, building your bed is a relatively simple process.

You will need:

- laundry (clean or dirty)
- a door

CLOTHING ITEM		BEST SUITED FOR ...
dressing gowns/towels		Dogs of all fur types. Terrycloth is the universal bedding material of choice – the perfect balance of thickness, softness, and malleability.
jeans		Nothing. Rigidity of denim creates uncomfortable edges when crumpled up.
flannel shirts		Long-haired dogs only. An ample fur buffer is needed to prevent chafing. Flannel is very itchy in direct contact with skin.
T-shirts		Best for short-haired, tiny dogs. Thin jersey material very comfortable but provides little padding for dogs over 15 lb.
suits		Not particularly comfortable for any dog, but there's something magical about knowing you're snoozing on a £1,000 Italian suit.
sweatshirts		Great material for all dogs, but paws may get stuck in hoods and pouches of many sweatshirts if beds are not constructed carefully.
underwear/ bras/ socks		Using undergarments can create a bedding potpourri of textures and padding densities, but these beds can also fall apart rather easily. Underwear beds are not recommended for dogs prone to chase dreams, as they may kick apart the construction during sleep.

Building a Bed out of Your Owner's Laundry

PROCURING YOUR
BUILDING MATERIALS

If the laundry you want to use is clean and folded, you'll have to wait for an ideal moment to make your bed. This moment occurs in the narrow window of time between when your owner folds his clothes and when he puts his clothes in a dresser or wardrobe. Locate the stacks of folded laundry and crash into them so they topple over.

Once you've demolished the tower of laundry, it's time to dishevel. With your teeth, clamp down on each item and shake vigorously.

Dirty laundry can streamline your construction significantly since  the clothing is already pre-tousled. If you're lucky enough to have an owner who simply leaves his dirty clothes on the floor, there's no need to rip open a laundry bag or tip over a laundry basket!

BUILDING YOUR BED

When you've gathered as much laundry as you want to use for your bed, you'll need to compress the clothes into a cohesive chunk. To do this, place all the clothes in a loose pile in front of a door that is ajar. Then go to the other side and push the door with your nose until you can't go any farther.

Now that you've formed the laundry into a solid block, move it to your desired location and leap on top of it. If you've constructed your laundry pile correctly, it should support your weight and naturally mould to your shape.

Consider decorating your space with personal effects such as a favourite toy or a beloved torn-up towel, and don't be afraid to add storage spaces for stolen table scraps, owner's jewellery, or mobile phone chargers.

That's it! You've done it! Since this process is so exhausting, take a well-earned nap, and don't be surprised if the sleep you get on a custom-built bed is the best you've ever had. After all, nobody knows what kind of bed you like better than you!

A Brief History of Dogs
in Man Wars

❖

Every day, dogs fight to defend their own territory, but there have been times when dogs have been pulled into the conflicts of humans. Sometimes it was for the good. At other times it was not. But every time it was for food.

Dogs have fought alongside man for ages, and throughout several cultures. There are records of dogs being used by the Egyptians, the Greeks and the Romans (who adopted an English breed with the awe-inspiring name the War Dog of Britannia). Attila the Hun, one of the most fearsome human warriors in history, used dogs in battle, no doubt making him even more fearsome.

The problem is that, while their use has been noted throughout history, the brave war dogs were rarely properly honoured. No historians took the time to scratch them under the chin and tell their side of the story. That has changed in the twenty-first century. These are, we believe, three of the most inspirational true tales of wartime canine heroism.

Stubby

The trenches of the First World War were a dreary, muddy, inhospitable place for soldiers. Into this bleak setting an American named John Robert Conroy smuggled his courageous mixed-breed dog Stubby. While Stubby was there he received a wound from a German grenade in the line of duty. He was sent to the rear for medical treatment, where his very presence and demeanour cheered up other wounded soldiers.

When he returned to the front line he was hit with poison gas, but Stubby was too tough to give up. Instead, he learned how to identify poison-gas attacks, and subsequently used his knowledge to warn the human soldiers when it was being employed against them. He also used his nose to locate wounded soldiers so that they could be brought back to safety. His acute sense of hearing let him know when an artillery shell was incoming before humans could, and he would warn soldiers when they should take cover. As if all that weren't bravery enough, he helped capture a spy. How many humans can make that claim?

For all his efforts, he was promoted to Sergeant Stubby. That is correct. If they could have understood him, Sergeant Stubby would have been able to give orders to lower-ranking humans. He was also given several medals, including the Wound Stripe (the First World War version of the Purple Heart), the Yankee Division YD Patch and the Republic of France Grande War Medal. After the war Sergeant Stubby was smuggled back home, where he met several presidents and won the first annual American Legion Convention Medal. He wore his medals proudly when he was in the public eye, but mostly preferred running around without them because they clanked too much.

Chips

Any dog can be a hero. When the Axis powers (bad guys) attacked the United States (good guys) during the Second World War, the U.S. responded by forming the Dogs for Defense. People across the country donated their dogs to the war effort, and these dogs bravely stepped up to help. In Pleasantville, New York, an Alsatian/Collie/Husky mongrel named Chips was enlisted to serve his country, but no one was aware of the appointment with greatness Chips had to keep overseas.

Chips travelled the world, serving as a tank guard dog in Europe and Africa. On one occasion Chips was with a platoon that was pinned down under enemy fire. The soldiers attached a phone wire to his collar and sent him back to base, thereby enabling them to call for back-up.

On another occasion Chips and his handler were attacked from a disguised sniper's hole during an early-morning stroll on a beach in Sicily. Amidst the chaos, Chips valiantly broke loose from his handler and leapt into the pillbox. One can only imagine what barking and biting Chips subjected them to, because shortly after he entered, the enemies fled their hole and surrendered. Despite sustaining some injuries, he returned to duty that night and alerted his platoon to an approaching Italian squad, who were then easily captured. He won a Purple Heart and a Silver Star for valour, and became the most decorated dog in the Second World War.

Bruiser

Vietnam was a bad place for man and dog alike. No one knew who the enemy was, or where they were, and it made everyone very tense. This did not make any of them, dog or man, less heroic. A lot of brave dogs were trained to sniff out the enemy in tunnels. It was dark and wet work, but it saved a lot of human lives.

One such dog, an Alsation named Bruiser, was being taken by his handler, John Flannelly, through a rice paddy near Da Nang. Suddenly, Bruiser stopped and signalled silently that the enemy was near by. His handler opened fire and was soon surrounded by whizzing bullets and explosions. Several of these explosions hit Bruiser's handler. Flannelly tried to send Bruiser back, but Bruiser was a Marine through and through, and he knew the meaning of Semper Fi. Under fire, he grabbed his handler and dragged him 300 metres, back to a helicopter that flew them both to safety.

Bruiser went to visit his handler in hospital and lifted his spirits. Bruiser didn't ask for any reward or special treatment. Like all courageous dogs in combat, he was just doing his duty as a dog and a soldier.

Tracking

———————❖———————

Smell something? Of course you do. That nose of yours is working constantly, picking up so many different scents that it's hard to keep them all straight. Human body odour crossed with Ralph Lauren Polo deodorant, charcoal smoke followed by the savoury aroma of barbecuing steaks, car exhaust/dead hedgehog mix – it's all coming to you in waves. Dogs with longer noses tend to have the best sense of smell, but all breeds are superior to humans.

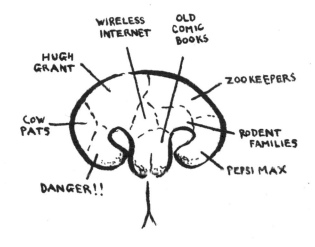

Smell Receptors of Your Nose

As good as it is, our great olfactory ability can be further refined. With proper development it can be used to isolate and follow a single scent in a technique called tracking. This ancient tradition involves 'getting on' a particular odour and then 'staying on' it until you locate the bearer.

It is an impressive skill to perfect that begins with respect for your quarry. As with everything, mastery is achieved through practice, practice, lying down for a few hours, maybe eating something, and then more practice.

Fear not if you are a dog that does not have much opportunity to get outside and train. There are ways to practise indoors. You will then be ready if the day comes when you are outside and called upon.

A nice easy target to start with is a misplaced television remote control. It is unable to move under its own power but is usually in motion quite a bit nonetheless. Your owner will be amazed and appreciative when you successfully produce it for him.

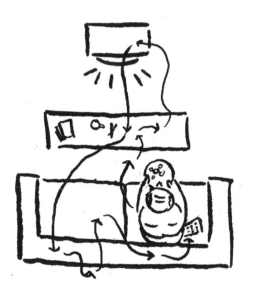

All dogs can track with a certain degree of success, but some breeds are better at it instinctually than others, who have to work harder to gain a full command of the art. It will require discipline, effort, and perhaps advanced training with a Master.

Tracking techniques are not infallible, and scents can be fleeting. While tracking, you need to be focused on the scent being followed at all times. Success will come with failure, opponents will best you, but the most important thing to keep in mind is that you should never accept defeat.

There will be times when a quarry eludes you because he simply is more skilled. A fox is a particularly cunning foe. As a species, they have a long lineage and familiarity with the dark ways of disappearance. One minute they are seemingly within reach and the next they are gone, having disappeared apparently into thin air. You are left to scratch your head and ponder how they did it. Remember, your opponent has only false trails and illusions, behind which he hides his true intentions. If you are on an organized hunt, take a minute to think about what went wrong while your owner adjusts his tweed jacket.

The value of tracking is not limited to a hunting situation, where combat with another animal is usually the end result. It can also be for the benefit of humankind. A lost child deserves to be found. A skilled tracking dog can locate one faster and more effectively than any human being. However, a tracker of the highest order does not simply find his quarry; he also ensures his tracking is done with honour. It is not

enough just to find the child; you must make certain another does not suffer the same misfortune.

It is said that the journey of a thousand miles must begin with a single step. Upon reaching a high level of proficiency you may be ready to try a most difficult pursuit. This exercise will probably frustrate and vex you, but upon its completion you will be uniquely qualified. Those who can find a fly by its scent can find any trail that has run dry.

What starts as a smell becomes a scent, and what begins as a trail becomes a path. Tracking is an ongoing journey that only ends when you stop sharpening your nose.

Courageous Dogs in History – Part Three
The Right Stuff

❖

In the mid-twentieth century, the Americans and Russians were in a race to see who would be the first to mark space as their territory. People in both countries desperately wanted to explore the heavens, but since they didn't know what they would find they were scared to go. And when people are too scared to do something, they get dogs to do it. Courageous, fearless, brave-hearted dogs.

BELKA AND STRELKA:
Pioneering Cosmo-Mutts

Belka and Strelka weren't the first mutts in space. That honour goes to a pup named Laika. Laika was very brave and gave her life to the cause of the Russian space programme, but Belka and Strelka didn't have to. These two dogs blasted off on 19 August 1960 in *Sputnik 2*. And they weren't alone. Their ship was a veritable Noah's Ark, carrying one grey rabbit, two rats from Moscow, some flies and forty mice. They orbited for the day, helping scientists learn more about weightlessness, space suits, and what mice talk about in space (mainly football and cheese). The whole crew survived the trip, and Belka and

Strelka came back down to earth with a few new tricks (weightless fetch, anyone?) and a lot of crazy stories to tell their friends at parties. The two street mutts became instant celebrities in their native Russia, and were featured on postage stamps in several countries. Both lived long healthy lives, and Strelka even had puppies. One of those puppies was called Pushinka, and she was given to Caroline Kennedy by Nikita Khrushchev. Pushinka's descendants are still alive today, and none of their owners understands why their dogs are always so interested in the weather conditions at Cape Canaveral.

FARLEY: 'One Small Step for Dogs – One Giant Leap for Dogkind'

Farley always dreamed big. When the other puppies in his litter were learning how to fetch, Farley was in the shed in the back garden,

tinkering with gadgets and fuses, trying to work out how to make bones sail up through the sky.

All day long he thought about space, and all night long he stared up at the stars. Other dogs made fun of his do-it-yourself rocket kits and protective goggles. But Farley didn't care if he was 'cool'. The little dog from a South Bend, Indiana farm knew he was destined for greatness. He just didn't know where he would find it. One warm summer's evening in 1969 he found out.

On 21 July of that year, the whole world watched as Neil Armstrong and Buzz Aldrin became the first human beings to ever set foot on the moon. Farley watched, too. As his owners and their friends applauded, Farley howled with approval. He had never been so proud to be an American. Even after the guests had quietened down, Farley kept howling at the men on the television. His owner got angry and told Farley to knock it off, but Farley didn't stop. Congratulating our American heroes was important! Then the phone calls from the neighbours started coming in, but that didn't make any difference to Farley either. He just kept on howling. A guest threw a shoe at him, but he missed because he hadn't taken any time to learn about trajectory and wind resistance the way Farley had.

After about twenty minutes his owner finally changed the channel. When that didn't quieten Farley either, the owner turned the television off altogether. None of that mattered one iota to Farley. He knew what he had seen, and what he was howling about. Man had set foot on the moon, and he wanted the whole world to know about his best friend's accomplishment.

After Farley was sent outside, he howled his congratulations directly up at the men on the moon for another twenty minutes without interruption, and didn't stop until astronaut Neil Armstrong, who could hear him all the way up there, personally thanked Farley for his support and politely asked him to keep it down.

How to Ruin the
Perfect Dinner Party

❖

Visitors! Who doesn't love them? They show up out of nowhere, give us lots of attention and petting, and if we're lucky they're loaded with treats!

Even better is a whole bunch of visitors. That's a party. Parties can really work out for you, especially if it's a garden barbecue or a match night party where plates full of pork pies are knocked to the floor when the commentator yells, 'No goal – the linesman signalled offside!'

However, there's one time when having a party isn't so great and that's called a dinner party.

Dinner-party visitors are different from normal visitors. They are known as guests. They're usually from the place where your owner works, or they're some idiots from up the street he's trying to impress. These people never have treats and they smell terrible, as if they've bathed in an awful cocktail of rubbing alcohol and lavender.

You might sense that a dinner party is about to take place if your owner becomes nervous and starts to Hoover obsessively. Your toys get put away. The throw rug on the couch disappears, and, even worse, gets washed. Your owner seems to be doing everything he can to remove your scent from the house – *your* house – making you feel like a stranger. And all for the benefit of some guests.

Who has any use for such guests? Certainly not you!

If your owner is having a dinner party, you must do everything in your power to ruin it.

Inevitably, your owner will try to shut you up in the spare bedroom before one of these abominations, but it is imperative that you do not allow him to do so. Owners always keep important stuff in their spare bedrooms like diplomas and Beatles commemorative plates. Make it clear that, should you be imprisoned in this space during the dinner party, these precious possessions will be in peril.

If you manage to negotiate your freedom, play it cool. Toppling over a punch bowl straight away will just get you locked up in the spare bedroom, valuables be damned. You must be subtle.

Start with some mingling. Keep it light and friendly. Anyone wearing a dark fabric that has a knack for attracting dog hair, such as black velvet, should get your special attention.

Next, set your sights on a lady guest. Discreetly make your way to the one in the most elegant outfit and lie down on the floor. Now let loose a foul cloud of flatulence. It's important you do this quietly. No blasters. If you feel another one coming on later, seek the same woman out again before letting it rip. The pay-off's better if you're consistent.

Select a male guest in your midst, preferably one with soft woollen suit trousers. Approach him casually and try to get him to pet you. When he brushes you aside, carefully mount his leg and begin a gentle humping. He will chuckle a bit and try to move you away, but don't be deterred. Keep it going and increase the intensity. Before he forcefully pushes you off and walks away, his manhood should be screaming.

Now that you've attended to a few individual guests, it's time to focus on the dinner party as a whole. This involves being keenly aware of when your owner is busy in the kitchen.

If your owner has a serving hatch, it's likely that appetizers have been placed on it – usually a selection of cheeses, some bread, perhaps an olive dip. When there is at least one guest present, lift yourself up and methodically lick every offering. If by chance there's some parma ham up there, make sure to grab some. You need to keep your energy up.

Now is the time for your first big play. Calmly make your way to the centre of the living room, throw your legs up high, and give your nether regions a good cleansing. For some reason, guests find well-washed genitals upsetting. This brings you closer to your objective, and you get some grooming done in the process!

At this point one of the guests should start to complain of a headache and indicate that he or she needs to leave. Our bet's on the elegantly dressed lady. That's a start, but your goal is to ensure none of these horrible people ever come to your house again.

While your owner is occupied in the dining room with soup and conversation, it's time to get some work done in the kitchen. By now he should have set the main course on the counter to rest. It will smell wonderful, but be warned, it could be wearing booties. Don't let this deter you. It's just some sick thing guests get off on. Making as little noise as you can, grab that meat and hightail it out of there.

Now race down to the master bedroom with your main course and leap onto the bed. As is the custom with humans, your owner will have requested that his guests place their coats there. Destroy them. Destroy them all.

Rest assured, you shall never see these guests again.

How to Ruin the Perfect Dinner Party

Creative Pee Stains

❖

Pee stains are beautiful expressions of canine artistry, and articulating the imagination through a visual medium like urine can enrich the life of even the most sedentary hound. The stains you create can range from the comical to the profound. As long as you put your heart, soul and pee into it, your art will be beautiful. Having an appreciation for fine art is just as important as mastering fetch or treeing squirrels. Being well-rounded, cultured creatures is what separates us from the lower species.

Many young pups look at the classic works of the Italian Greyhound masters or even the primitive pee stains found on the bottom part of the Lascaux cave walls and think they couldn't possibly create the same kind of visual splendour, but that's not true. All creative pee stains start with the same basic techniques. Once you've learned the fundamentals, you can begin to forge your own personal style. With that in mind, here are a few ideas and instructions to get you started.

BEGINNER LEVEL STAINING: The Butterfly

This design is simple and elegant. The basis for all artistic stains is arse-wiggling control. Learning to manipulate your lower body is essential. Don't worry if your first few designs don't match the pictures here. Just drink some more water and keep practising until you've got it right!

1. Choose a floor surface with some texture. Thick, solid-white carpet is best.
2. Squat and dispense. As you pee, wiggle your bottom in a 'figure of eight' motion.

3. Finish with a straight line down the centre of the eight to form the thorax and abdomen. The antennae should form naturally as the pee seeps into the carpet.

4. Step back and enjoy your work! Congratulations, you just made art for the first time!

5. Bonus step: To really make your butterfly soar, smear some dirt on the wings, starting from the thorax and dragging outwards.

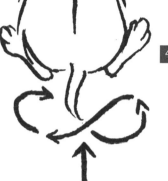

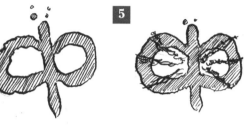

INTERMEDIATE LEVEL STAINING: The Christmas Tree

This design requires great control, but if you can master the technique you'll be able to create a beautiful piece of art that's perfect for the holiday season.

1. Go outside. This design is meant for crisp green lawns only. Grass is the canvas upon which you will create your masterpiece. If there is snow on the ground, scoop it aside, eat it, or roll around in it until it melts.

2. First, create your outline for the tree by tearing up a line of grass in a triangle shape.

3. To make the stump for your Christmas tree, dig out a large square patch underneath the base of your grass triangle.

4. Now it's time to decorate your tree. Starting from the base of the triangle, pee thin, curved lines from side to side.

5. You've drawn on your string of Christmas lights, but don't forget the star at the top! Unless you're a big breed like a Great Dane, Newfoundland or Irish Wolfhound, you'll probably need to take a break and refill your bladder. Have another bowl of water. Once you're ready to pee again, go to the top of your triangle and let loose. Really let it gush. You want the star to burst with rays of light.

6. You won't see full results immediately following your creative urination. All you will see is your original triangle of grass and an earthy stump, but be patient. The nitrogen and ammonia in your pee take a few hours to take effect, but when they do – look out, Picasso! Soon your pee will create a radiant pattern on the lawn that your owners will surely treasure through the holidays.

ADVANCE LEVEL STAINING: The Pollock

In November 2006, one of the artist Jackson Pollock's paintings, *No. 5, 1948* sold for a record $140 million. If you've progressed far enough in your training as an artist, you might be ready to re-create his master-piece on the walls of your own home. This stain requires great balance and expert pee control. While we would never suggest that bitches are not as qualified to make this stain, male dogs may find it slightly easier since it relies heavily on leg lifting.

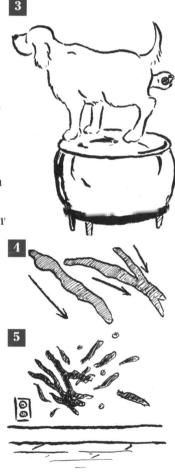

1. Find a blank, non-wallpapered wall of the house.
2. Push something you can stand on against the wall. The platform should give you at least two feet of extra height. Ottomans, upside-down buckets or twenty-four-inch TVs all work well.
3. What makes this pee stain so difficult is the movement required. As you pee with your back right leg lifted, you must con-tinuously bend and straighten your other three legs. This creates the sense of movement and flow in the final stain.
4. With your leg lifted, begin making diag-onal pee streaks – always going top to bottom. Repeat.
5. Remember that the real artistry in this pee stain comes out in the form of com-position. Think about spacing, streak orientation and drizzle variation. If you work hard enough on your craft, who knows how many bones one of your pieces could fetch at an auction?

The Lost Art of the Pheasant Hunt

If you've ever caught the scent of pheasant on the breeze and felt something stirring deep inside you, there is a reason. Once, when people hunted for their food, the dog was valued more highly than gold. A revered retriever could find a felled fowl and bring it back, or retrieve it, so that it might be prepared for the evening's repast. There's nothing like the feeling that you are providing for your owner, and a little something for yourself.

Sadly, the popularity of pheasant hunting is now at an all-time low. If you do get a chance to go out pheasant hunting, you should jump at the opportunity to experience the tradition. You get to be outside, without a lead, hanging around with your owner and just enjoying nature. While some dogs are better equipped than others to sniff out a downed fowl through a tall patch of reeds, any dog can do it.

1. Equipment

Fig. 1:
The ideal fowl-retrieval
equipment

You will need yourself and your snout. That's all!

2. Preparations

Fig. 2:
A good night's rest

A good fowling dog should be prepared to go at a moment's notice. Realistically, though, you will not be hunting pheasants or quail at a moment's notice. Most humans only hunt pheasants and partridges when the leaves have fallen from the trees and the birds fly overhead in large groups. Even those signs are not enough to get your hopes up. Rather, wait until you see that your owners have laid out their nicest clothes and a large, hollow stick that smells faintly of rotten eggs.

When you see these things, get a good night's rest, because the odds are good that you will spend tomorrow in a cold, glorious place.

Fig. 3:
Signs that a game hunt
will take place

3. The Hunt

Your hunting grounds

Patience is a large part of the pheasant hunt. Even though you have done your part by being ready immediately, you will have to endure the long wait of having your owner blearily making coffee because he's awake three hours earlier than usual. But once he's dressed and has filled his enormous mug with coffee, the hunt is on! Well, first there's a ride, which, if you can believe it, is only the tip of the iceberg.

When you finally arrive at the designated hunting spot, prepare to sit still for hours at a time. This can be especially challenging, particularly when you are in the middle of the countryside and wanting to play around with your owner and some of his friends, but the pay-off is worth it. Use this time to stay alert and watch the sky closely for birds.

Eventually a pheasant will fly overhead. This is when the owner will lift up his stick and point it at the bird. When the stick barks, DO NOT RUN! This is very important. Bravery in the face of loud noises is yet another important aspect of the pheasant hunt. Even though the noise is like thunder, which can be frightening, it is just your owner's way of telling the pheasant that it should fall from the sky.

If a pheasant is disobedient and does not fall, you should stay put and look sympathetically at your owner, who will be angry. If a bird does fall from the sky, this is your chance to spring into action. Watch the

No!   *Yes.*

pheasant fall. By the time it gets halfway to the ground, use your innate dog trigonometry to work out where it landed. Take off immediately for the spot where you have determined it will be. With your best game-sniffing nose, root that pheasant out. Grasp it gingerly by the neck and take it back to your owner.

If more than one pheasant falls, don't be greedy. Take one bird back to your owner, then go back for more.

Hopefully, one pheasant will not mark the end of your hunting excursion. Return to your waiting position and prepare to bring back more bounty. At the end of the day, when you are safely back at home, you can sleep soundly in the knowledge that you have done a great job helping stock the fridge while spending a great day in the outdoors.

You are rewarded for your patience

Training a New Human

The addition of a new human to the home can be stressful for any dog. Sometimes an owner will bring home a mate that does not know the spot where you like to be scratched. At other times your owners will disappear in a panic for a few days, only to come back with a tiny third human. No matter what the situation, a new human in the home comes with a great deal of responsibility. They need to be taught when to feed you, when to walk you, where your toys are kept, and, in the case of tiny humans, why they shouldn't pull your tail.

In the end, though, training a new human is always worth the effort. A well-trained human makes a better, more loving companion. They can almost predict your needs. If you don't spend the necessary time early on, you will pay for it later with a human that is lazy and uncooperative. Taking the time now will result in a better relationship and a happier human.

1. ASSERT YOURSELF

Right from the start, you must make sure your new human knows his place. To do this, assert your dominance. He must know that you are in charge. When the new human comes to you and pats you on the head, stare into his eyes without looking away. If he says 'Aah!' and rubs your ears, you will know that he is ready to be trained.

2. MAKE YOUR NEEDS CLEAR

Most new humans will not intuitively understand your routine, so it is important that you communicate as clearly and effectively as possible. Start with something simple. When you want to go out, you can bark at your new human as much as you want, but if he doesn't understand barking you aren't going to get anywhere. Instead, stand by the door and look sadly at him. If he walks by without pausing, scratch at the door and whine. Grabbing your lead and holding it out to him should be enough of a sign for most humans to pick up on. If your new human is still unable to comprehend what you want, knock something that looks important off a table. This will send the message loud and clear.

3. PATIENCE

A new human has the mind of a puppy. If he shoves you out of bed at night only to climb in himself, you need to understand that he gets tired, too, and may not be thinking straight. Just jump right back on the bed. If he shoves you off the bed again, don't get discouraged. Just wait until he is asleep and get back up there. Eventually he will learn that he is only in your bed because you – generously – let him stay.

4. SPEND TIME WITH THEM

The key to dealing with humans is familiarity. The more familiar a human is with you, the more likely he is to accept your commands. Don't be afraid to run up to him on occasion or follow him around. This reinforces the notion that you are now a constant presence in his life that he needs to consider, as well as ensuring that you get more scratching.

5. REPETITION

Just because a human does something right once doesn't mean that he will always do it. He needs to be shown how to do something several times before it becomes second nature. If he doesn't seem to know where the treats are, stand right by the spot where they are kept. Look excited every time he approaches you. If that doesn't work, stand on your hind legs and put your paws near the treats, panting lightly and hungrily to drive the message home. These cues should make it sufficiently clear to him that you would like a treat. As soon as you have finished devouring your treat, go through the whole routine again. This is the only way to make sure the new human has learned the lesson.

6. BARK, BUT DON'T BITE

On the surface, biting is the most direct and effective way to convey your message to someone. If a child pulls your tail or tries to ride you like a horse, a bite will certainly set it straight, but in the long run it will derail any plans you might have of one day getting that child to chase you around the garden or throw a ball for you. Remember, biting is the first reaction of a ruffian. Instead, just bark loudly. It conveys the same message without the lasting negative impact. Remember: scold, don't scar.

7. REWARD THEM

If he does something right, make sure he knows you appreciate it. When he takes you for a good walk, show your appreciation by wagging your tail and displaying your tummy to him so he can enjoy the sensation of giving you a good rub. This is beneficial to you, too, because you get a tummy rub out of it. There is no downside here.

Performing

Dogs perform tricks as a means to an end. We're not typically in it for the art. We do it for the pay-off, which usually takes the form of a substantial food treat or extra-special attention. Some dogs will even take a walk as payment. The point is that once a dog reaches a certain level, what he charges is really up to the individual performer. The good news is that the sky seems to be the limit.

It's very difficult to perform and manage your career at the same time. You need to spend time honing your craft, not booking gigs. Owners can open doors for you in this business that no other human can. If you're lucky enough to have a savvy owner, he will put you on the path to stardom, a journey which hopefully ends with you being tossed steaks and petted by appreciative people whose hands smell like steak.

To achieve that station in life takes work, a little skill and a lot of luck. First you have to learn the basics, beginning with 'the Three Ss': Sit, Shake and Stay.

Sit, Shake and Stay

Nobody begins their career headlining at the Albert Hall. You have to start somewhere, and this is the place. The Three Ss are very easy to learn and execute. The first two, Sit and Stay, are basically the same thing. They may seem overdone and trite, but you need the Three Ss in your act. They're the basis for many advanced tricks, and some fool in the audience will always want to see them. Don't worry, you'll get to perform stuff with more razzmatazz in no time.

Ambitious dogs can go to the next step, taking the time to expand their act with tricks that are done on the ground:

Down, Roll Over and Play Dead

These can really jazz up your act. Ground tricks are not new by any means, but they do represent a higher level of craft than the Three Ss and are rewarded as such. Ground tricks play well in Cleethorpes and they can get you some serious extra belly rubbing. To get all the mileage you can out of them, do each at slow, medium and fast speeds.

At some point your owner is going to run out of tricks for you to perform, and as a result your career is likely to stall. Without new material even the most talented performer begins to flounder. This is the perfect time to take your act to the next level by incorporating your owner.

Ventriloquism is a great way to do this. It's similar to the old 'whisper' gag where you 'speak' quietly, except here the aim is not to move your jaw at all. It takes time to perfect. Try practising in front of a mirror and you'll get it eventually. Then work up a routine with your owner. It works best if you play the straight man and let him have all the juiciest lines.

No act is complete without a grand finale. Mathematics is perhaps the best turn of them all. To do it correctly you need an accomplished owner. This is one where he has to have some performing talent. You don't want your finale falling flat.

The trick begins with your owner asking you a maths question. It does not matter what it is. Let him decide. As with all tricks, he will be holding some form of treat. As soon as he poses the question, begin to paw the floor very slowly and deliberately, keeping your eyes on the treat the entire time.

If he has what it takes, your owner will count up one number each time your paw strikes the floor and present you the treat at precisely the right time. Knocking an audience dead with this trick never gets old.

Upon mastery of mathematics, you have made the big time. Break a leg! Make sure you enjoy every moment.

Park Legends

---❖---

You've read about some awesome feats of will and bravery in these pages. Alas, very few of us have opportunities for such thrilling triumphs. Your owner probably doesn't get out much, let alone end up trapped on a mountain peak so that you could use your body heat to keep him alive. And his boy-child isn't idiot enough to need saving from a climb into a ravine full of broken glass and adders. Now if you'd be allowed to drive the car more often, perhaps you could get yourself up to the Highland wilderness for some proper derring-do.

Until then, you can always try to wow 'em a little closer to home.

Who among us hasn't longed for that one true day in the sun? You take decisive action, and suddenly time stops. Frisbees clatter to the earth as your peers and their companions look upon you in awe, a moment that will linger in their memories. Your owner gazes at you with pride. Well, that may not be pride, but attention's attention.

We all have it within us to achieve greatness in the park. Perhaps these legendary tales can inspire you.

10 MAY 1992, BRAINTREE, ESSEX: Tor, a Bulldog, was a known loner. He was never one for chase. Tor preferred to sit in one spot and stare at a patch of tangled weeds near the human water fountain. Sometimes he would slurp the air, but mostly he stared. No one quite knew what to make of him. A tennis ball would roll his way. He'd give it a sniff, slurp, and keep on staring. One day the patch of weeds he stared at was gone. Rumours of his amazing ocular shearing abilities have swirled ever since, and proud long-haired breeds give Tor a wide berth to this day.

7 JUNE 2003, VIRGINIA WATER: A Pomeranian named Valentino had some big problems with the park lawn sprinkler. Whenever he tried to get a drink from a nearby puddle, it would start smacking him around. Not

one to take any nonsense, Valentino fought back, spending all day barking and biting at the water the sprinkler shot at him. These skirmishes raged for a month. The sprinkler hissed and spat. Valentino yipped and snapped. But on this Saturday, Valentino really gave it to the sprinkler. Then, suddenly, the water ceased to be. Triumphant, Valentino strutted over to his owner and was rewarded with cooing and a treat. Some don't believe, whispering that the sprinkler was just on a timer. But those who were there swear that little Valentino drank all the sprinkler's water that day.

21 JULY 1998, BLACKBURN, LANCASHIRE: Hugo, a Whippet alleged to have crashed and burned in the show profession, took off with his owner's ham sandwich, ruined a game of bowls, knocked over a large jug of orange drink, snatched a Barbie doll and discarded its gnawed headless body in a patch of brambles, ignited a small fire by toppling a grill, and caused an entire junior football team to cry. Hugo's path of destruction has yet to be rivalled.

27 AUGUST 2001, LEEDS: Ken, a Japanese Akita, broke all previously held records by ingesting thirty-two deposits of dog droppings within an hour. Since then, an annual competitive Poo Eating Contest has taken place in our nation's parks every August Bank Holiday, but to this day no dog has managed to top Ken's phenomenal accomplishment.

4 SEPTEMBER 2006, CAITHNESS, SCOTLAND: While his owner was distractedly chatting up a lady owner, Mr Special, a rescue Terrier, is said to have dug a hole straight to China, where he successfully hid his much-loathed lead in the remote province of Guizhou.

The Greatest Scratching Position
in the World

———————————❖———————————

It is ancient; it is timeless. It has been known by many names. We call it the Jerry. What you call it is up to you, but one thing is clear – it is the greatest scratching position known to canines.

It is not difficult to perform. Anyone can do the Jerry. Once you know it, you will practically look forward to becoming itchy. You do not need to be young and frisky, or even flexible, to perform the Jerry. You are never too furry, too chubby, or too old to learn how to do it. The Jerry has always been, and will always be.

The Jerry is many things to many dogs and all things to all dogs. To prepare for it, you need only open yourself to the universe. Only when you welcome the possibility of the Jerry will the Jerry come to you. To do this, it is very important to rid your being of every ounce of tension. Luckily, this is usually pretty easy for a dog.

Become calm. Any residual anger you feel towards the groomer or the dog walker will merely impede your progress and delay the Jerry. Live in the present. The only moment that matters is now.

Breathe deeply and naturally. Focus on relaxing. Eliminate distractions. If the doorbell rings, do not bark. If a cocky Pekingese struts past your garden, remain calm. Remain centered. Allow him to pass. These are trivialities. They cannot affect the eternal Jerry.

Don't try to pretend the itch isn't there. It is. Accept that you have an itch, and that it is in a spot you can't reach, and that it's really, really itchy. But it won't be for long.

Remember, do not force the Jerry. Allow the Jerry. You Jerry without doing.

It will take some dogs many years to learn, and it will take other dogs only minutes, but once you have alerted the universe that you are ready, you have done all there is to do. Now all you have to do is wait for the Jerry to come to you. The Jerry may be hard to describe, but you'll know it when you feel it, because there is nothing else in the world that feels as good as this:

Dog Tags

Hey! **You read a whole book without eating it first! That deserves a special treat.** Here is a tag you can wear to show off all the knowledge you've gained.

Chasing

Swimming

Shoe Chewing

Costume Escape

Bone Burial

Pee Staining

Toy Construction

Tracking

*Owner
Embarrassment*

ACKNOWLEDGEMENTS

The authors would like to thank:

Victoria Skurnick, Daniel Greenberg, Bruce Tracy, Ryan Doherty, everyone at Levine-Greenberg and Random House/Villard; Emily Flake, Bob Stein and Rob Pesce.

We would also each like to thank:

JOE: The Garden, Strange, Garms and Kroll families, Jeff and Andrea Perry, Ivan Drucker, the staff of *The Onion*, and Jesse Thorn and The Sound of Young America.

JANET: My mom, Barbara Ginsburg; Harold Ginsburg, Matthew Ginsburg and the rest of the Ginsburg and Colmans families the world over, Camille Rose Garcia, Dennis Messner, Dana Glassburn, Jennifer Miya, all my supportive friends and my Dad.

CHRIS: Heather Sabin, Dale and Susan Pauls, Todd and Heather Pauls, the entire Pauls/Smith family, Matt Fink, Tom and Meghan Hendricks, Chris Briquelet and family, Alex Wilson, Blake Engeldorf, Jerard Adler, Ryan Pettersen, Jerry Ashworth, Jesse Hughes and everyone at the Laser Source, Inc.

SCOTT: Beryl and Leigh Sherman, Craig Thorn, Tim Kazurinsky, Joyce Sloane, David Miner, Greg Walter, Sam Means, Ed Herbstman, and Ella, Max, Willy, Maggie and Smash.

ANITA: Mum Maria & Pops David Serwacki, Pupka, Julianne Serwacki, Joan & Bob McDonald, the Camacho family, the Rose family and Kathy Kobler.

ABOUT THE AUTHORS

JOE GARDEN is the Features Editor for *The Onion*. He is also the co-author of *Citizen You! Helping Your Government Help Itself* and a writer for the forthcoming PBS educational cartoon *Word Girl*. He currently resides in Brooklyn, NY, with his wife, Anita Serwacki, and has had two dogs in his childhood, Phoebe and Sojourn.

JANET GINSBURG has worked as a field producer on *The Daily Show with Jon Stewart*, and is a former staff writer for *The Onion*. She has also written or produced programmes for the Discovery, Sci-Fi and E! Entertainment channels, and her work appears in publications such as *Vibe, Blender* and the *LA Weekly*. She has known and loved countless dogs, including Pogo, Aldo, Missy and Bucks. She lives in Brooklyn.

CHRIS PAULS is a contributing writer for *The Onion*. He lives in Middleton, Wisconsin.

ANITA SERWACKI is a contributing writer for *The Onion* and a writer for the PBS animated series *Word Girl*. She is also a well-known New York City DJ and served as music supervisor on the documentary *The Kid Stays in the Picture*. Anita grew up with an awesome Husky named Nyack who was a pro at escaping fenced-in areas, but who learned to ring the doorbell to get back in the house. She currently lives in Brooklyn, NY, with her husband and co-writer, Joe Garden.

SCOTT SHERMAN is a contributing writer for *The Onion* and a staff writer for its online video channel, The Onion News Network. He has also written for the *New York Times Magazine*'s Funny Pages and the A&E television network. He lives in New York City with his hound mix, Ella.

ABOUT THE ILLUSTRATOR

EMILY FLAKE is an illustrator, cartoonist and author. She is the creator of the cartoon strip Lulu Eightball, which runs in alternative news weeklies across the USA, and the author of *These Things Ain't Gonna Smoke Themselves*. She lives in Brooklyn with a man almost, but not quite, fuzzy enough to be a puppy. She likes boxing and knitting and pie.

This book is set in Cheltenham, a typeface originally conceived as a book type by Bertram Goodhue, a considerable American architect. As Alexander Lawson wrote in his *Anatomy of a Typeface*, 'In the post-World War II era, when its use declined, it became the subject of numerous articles in printing-trade periodicals, most expressing divided opinions on its pedigree as a good letter form or its usefulness as a typeface.' What better face to use than one that brings up discussions of pedigree? Whether for thoroughbreds or mutts, Chelt does the job.